ZWEIG WHITE & ASSOCIATES

INSIDER'S GUIDE *to* Mergers & Acquisitions for A/E/P & Environmental Consulting firms

George E. Christodoulo
Executive Editor

Molly O. Whelan
Managing Editor

Contributors—Susan M. Barnard, Dana C. Blakslee, George E. Christodoulo, Jonathan D. Gatti, Mark J. Goodale, Philip C. Horowitz, Michael E. Morrissey, Robert C. Rives, Jr., Martin B. Shulkin, Norman C. Spector, Melvin A. Warsaw, Molly O. Whelan, Frederick D. White, and Mark C. Zweig

ZWEIG WHITE & ASSOCIATES, INC.
NATICK, MASSACHUSETTS
SAN FRANCISCO, CALIFORNIA

Printed in the U.S.A.

ISBN 1-885002-30-0

Also Available from Zweig White & Associates:
The DOT Market for A/E/P & Environmental Consulting Firms
The Health Care Market for A/E/P & Environmental Consulting Firms
Valuation Survey of A/E/P & Environmental Consulting Firms
Policies, Procedures & Benefits Survey of A/E/P & Environmental Consulting Firms
Marketing Survey of A/E/P & Environmental Consulting Firms
Principal's Survey of A/E/P & Environmental Consulting Firms
Financial Performance Survey of Environmental Consulting Firms
Satellite Office Survey of A/E/P & Environmental Consulting Firms
Project Management Survey of A/E/P & Environmental Consulting Firms
Insider's Guide to SF254/255 Preparation
Insider's Guide to Cashing in on Your Equity, 2nd edition
Insider's Guide to Getting into Print
Insider's Guide to Professional Recruitment Secrets
Insider's Guide to Direct Marketing
Management Ideas That Work!
More Management Ideas That Work!
Even More Management Ideas That Work!
Still More Management Ideas That Work!
Revolutionary Marketing! A Video Seminar
The Zweig Letter (weekly management newsletter)
The Zweig Letter Audio Edition (monthly management audio newsletter)

Zweig White & Associates, Inc.
600 Worcester Street
Natick, Massachusetts 01760

tel (508) 651-1559
fax (508) 653-6522

info@zwa.com
http://www.zwa.com

Contents

Chapter 9: The Transaction Documents

- *The transaction documents, led by the Purchase & Sale Agreement (P&S), represent the final, written expression of the business deal.*

Chapter 10: The Closing and Integration

- *As the closing approaches, the transaction partners primarily focus on preparing for the closing and on the issues related to the integration of the two firms.*

Figures

Merger Mania

Just ten years ago, a merger or acquisition of an engineering or architectural consulting firm was fairly unusual. Now, hardly a week goes by that you don't hear or read of another merger across the country or down the street. With over 50,000 engineering, architecture, and environmental consulting firms in the U.S., this is a timely, universal subject that should be of interest to every size firm in the A/E/P and environmental industries—it's rare to find a firm that hasn't been approached by another company regarding a merger or sale. The implications of a merger or acquisition are enormous for every aspect of a firm's practice from marketing, to finance, to human resources and more, and every firm principal needs to have some plan of how they will react when an opportunity arises.

The *Insider's Guide to Mergers & Acquisitions* is a result of the collaboration between the attorneys of Burns & Levinson LLP and the consultants of Zweig White & Associates, combining the insights of seasoned attorneys and management consultants who make their livings assisting consulting engineering, architecture, and environmental consulting firms with ownership transition, and mergers and acquisitions.

The guide is organized to give you an understanding of how mergers and acquisitions unfold in our profession. Topics include what's driving the market, who the players are, and the steps to exploring, structuring, negotiating, completing, and implementing a merger or acquisition. Whether you're a buyer or a seller, you'll learn how to prepare your firm for a merger or acquisition, draft a letter of intent, conduct due diligence, prepare for closing and integration, and measure the success of your transaction. In addition, the guide contains important information about corporate and tax considerations, and specific transaction documents.

Like the previous *Insider's Guides,* the *Insider's Guide to Mergers & Acquisitions* is packed with samples, forms, checklists, examples, war stories, special tips, other resources, and much more. Our goal is to present, in a readable format with real-life examples, the complexity, risks, and rewards of buying or selling a firm.

This *Insider's Guide to Mergers & Acquisitions* is intended to give readers insight into how these deals are structured— after all, the more you know, the more successful your M&A endeavors will be. The information in this book, however, should be viewed as an introduction and overview of the very complex world of mergers and acquisitions. Throughout the text we encourage both buyers and sellers to get legal, accounting, insurance, and financial advice specific to their particular transaction—and every buyer or seller should take this advice seriously before embarking on any deal.

George E. Christodoulo
April 18, 1997

2
How to Make Your Firm "Transaction-Ready"
3
For Buyers
4
For Sellers
5
The Search Process and First Meeting
6
Corporate & Tax Considerations
7
The Letter of Intent
8
The Due Diligence Investigation
9
The Transaction Documents
10
The Closing and Integration

Chapter 1

Overview

☑ *As mergers and acquisitions become more and more common in the A/E/P and environmental consulting industries, it is important to understand how to plan for and participate in a deal. Although merger and acquisition transactions are complex, they are easier to understand when viewed as a series of cumulative chronological steps.*

Change is Afoot

Just ten years ago, a merger or acquisition of an engineering, architecture or environmental consulting firm was fairly unusual. Now it seems hardly a week goes by that you don't hear or read about another deal. One week it's an *ENR* Top 500 firm across the country. The next week it's your competitor down the street. Firms of all shapes and sizes are getting in on the action. Change is afoot in our profession, but what's driving it?

Demographics

Many architecture, engineering, and/or planning firms that began in the post-war era have reached maturity and their founders are preparing to retire, often without adequate ownership transition planning. As these principals "cash out," their firms may face a financial and managerial crisis— the only options may be to merge or go out of business.

Evolution From Practice to Business

The last 25 years have also seen a major transformation of the architecture and engineering professions from traditional technically-oriented "practices" to modern client-oriented businesses. Firms have adopted mainstream management methods in finance, marketing, human resources, and operations, including the use of strategic and opportunistic mergers and acquisitions to enter new markets or increase market share.

National and International Client Sophistication

The market for architecture, engineering, and environmental consulting services grows less provincial every day. Firms that once served a single county now find themselves working with clients in other states and partnering with other firms around the world. Sophisticated clients with national and international projects often look for "one stop shopping" for all their needs— and if you can't provide it, someone else will.

Volatility in the Environmental Consulting Sector

The meteoric rise of the environmental consulting industry from 1970 to 1993 launched thousands of new firms, and some were acquired by traditional architecture or engineering firms looking to enter the environmental market. But the end of the boom has forced a consolidation, and marginal firms have been absorbed. Environmental consulting leaders are using acquisitions to grow in a stagnant market, and aggressive smaller and mid-sized companies are jockeying to align themselves with larger partners.

Experience and Confidence

As increasing numbers of architecture, engineering, planning, and/or environmental firms complete mergers and acquisitions, they learn from their experiences— both good and bad. As an industry, we've gotten better at avoiding bad deals and getting the most out of good deals.

Opportunistic vs. Strategic Deals

In our experience, firms take two very different routes to considering a merger, sale, or acquisition. Some firms enter into opportunistic deals as they arise, and others plan more carefully for strategic deals.

Opportunistic Deals

One example of an opportunistic deal is the proverbial "fire sale." Neither the buyer nor the seller may have planned on this course, but fate brings them together at the right time. Sophisticated buyers can be very successful with the opportunistic approach, thanks to their experience in evaluating deals and companies.

Opportunistic sellers often short-change themselves, however, by responding to an unsolicited call from a potential buyer, entering into negotiations to "see what will happen," then consummating a deal before all options have been considered. In any case, with the number of business opportunities available today, every A/E/P or environmental consulting firm should have some plan of how to react when these possibilities arise.

Strategic Deals

Strategic deals begin when firms make a planned decision about the direction of their business and conclude that an acquisition or a sale may help them achieve their goals. These firms define their criteria for success as completely as possible, conduct a thorough search to uncover every firm that fits their profile, and then choose the best option available to them. In short, strategic buyers and sellers have a very clear idea of their goals and a better means of measuring success and failure.

Strategic buyers almost invariably begin the acquisition process for one of two reasons. Some seek to develop new services or client-types in their firm's existing geographic area. Others seek to export existing services to similar clients in a new geographic area. In some cases, a small acquisition is planned as an alternative to hiring or establishing a branch office from scratch.

Strategic sellers have their own objectives in considering deals. A sale may be planned as an alternative to internal ownership transfer. Frequently, an outside sale will yield the highest value with the most liquidity. In other cases, principals far from retirement age seek increased growth opportunities for their firm and its people through a strategic sale. These principals don't look at a sale as the end of the line, but rather an entry into their next stage of development.

This guidebook was created to help A/E/P and environmental consulting firms understand the process of buying, selling, and merging, so that they will be prepared to make the best decisions when the time comes.

Types of Transactions

There are three basic types of corporate transactions: acquisitions, mergers, and consolidations.

Acquisitions (Purchase and Sale)

In this form of transaction, the assets or the stock of one party (the seller) are purchased for cash and/or stock of the other party (the buyer). The buyer is clearly the dominant party in acquisition transactions. If the deal is structured as a purchase of the seller's stock, then the seller may continue to operate as an independent entity. If the transaction is a purchase of the assets of the seller, however, then the seller's identity as a separate entity is lost.

Mergers

The term "merger" refers to a technical form of corporate transaction in which two firms are combined through an exchange of stock (and possibly some cash and/or notes), and the buyer is the only surviving entity.

It is important to note that the name "merger" is often given to transactions that, in terms of tax and/or corporate purposes, are really not mergers. Sellers (and sellers' stockholders) may push to have the transaction called a merger for internal and external purposes— usually to avoid the stigma of being "the party sold." In the interest of promoting a smooth transaction in which the seller's clients will be retained, buyers may also support such a designation, even though the transaction is technically an acquisition.

Consolidations

A consolidation is a form of transaction where the two parties combine to form an entirely new third entity, which is the only survivor of the transaction.

The Parties

Throughout this book, the two parties to the transaction are described as the "buyer" and the "seller." The buyer is the more dominant party in the transaction and the seller is the party which will not survive as an independent entity after the transaction.

For the most part, the information in this guide pertains to the transaction and therefore is intended to assist both the buyer and the seller— and although we have clearly indicated (as in Chapters 3 and 4) which sections apply to only one party or the other, we recommend that both buyers and sellers read the entire book to understand the other party's expectations.

Branch Office Considerations

In the A/E/P and environmental consulting industries, there is significant opportunity to sell only a piece (or pieces) of your firm. You shouldn't close a branch office before you've explored the possibility of selling it. We have seen a number of firms successfully carve off one or more branch offices, a laboratory operation, or a subsidiary company to raise cash, reduce overhead, or allow management to concentrate on what it does best.

It is becoming more and more commonplace for firms to buy and sell branch offices— even an unproductive branch that seems to be going nowhere may bring multiple offers. Sometimes short-term cash flow problems prompt management to shut down a viable office, and an intermediary can often identify potential buyers with just a few phone calls.

Oftentimes firms headquartered in the same area as a target satellite office become buyers in order to seize the opportunity to add people and backlog. Or buyers may be firms from outside the area who have been looking for a way to enter the market or to expand there. And some opportunistic buyers just prefer branches to small, independent firms. Negotiating with an entrepreneur who's built his business from scratch can be like asking a mother to give away her baby. It can be much smoother to deal with a relatively dispassionate multi-office firm that judges only the business sense of a transaction.

International Deal Considerations

More and more often we are seeing international deals between companies of all sizes, and it may be that *your* strategic plan calls for expansion to another country at some point. If you are thinking about buying a foreign firm or selling your firm to a foreign company, however, there are a number of additional considerations you should keep in mind.

First, different cultures and languages make the search process more complex. International firms are generally more difficult to identify, because information sources are less readily available and less comprehensive. In addition, identifying the correct point of contact within the organization (president, regional director, or head of M&A) can sometimes turn into a science project.

The corporate and tax aspects of the merger or acquisition (in structuring the deal and after the transaction has been completed) will also be more complex with an international deal, than with a firm in the U.S. Depending on where the partner firm is located, it may also be more difficult and/or expensive to get to know the principals of the other firm, and to conduct a thorough due diligence investigation. Cultural differences and language barriers can make it more difficult for employees and principals to establish a good working relationship. You also have to plan for how you will protect yourself when the value of the currency used by your clients fluctuates— contracts may need to include provisions to accommodate such payment risks. Finally, there are also increased management challenges inherent in dealing with any remote location, challenges like coordinating communication over several time zones, structuring accounting systems to accommodate different currencies, and overcoming any "us versus them" attitude that might develop.

We have a few basic recommendations for firms who want to pursue an international transaction opportunity. First, find the right advisors— an attorney, accountant, management consultant, and liability insurance consultant (and financing source, if you're a buyer) with experience in the A/E/P or environmental consulting industry *and* in structuring an international deal. In addition, if your consultant is known to overseas firms, you will have an easier time getting

International Deal Considerations & Recommendations

Figure 1-1

Keep the following considerations and recommendations in mind if you're thinking of pursuing a transaction with an international firm.

Considerations

- Different cultures and languages make the search process more complex
- International firms are harder to identify— information sources are less comprehensive and less readily available
- Identifying the correct point of contact within the organization can be difficult
- Corporate and tax aspects are more complex
- More difficult and/or expensive to get to know the principals of the other firm
- More difficult and/or expensive to conduct due diligence
- Cultural differences and language barriers make it more difficult for employees and principals to establish good working relationships
- The value of the currency used by your clients may fluctuate
- Additional management challenges are inherent in dealing with any remote location

Recommendations

- Find an attorney, accountant, management consultant, liability insurance consultant, and financing source with industry *and* international experience
- Hire a consultant who is known internationally to help you get in the door
- Be aware of the challenges that might arise, and do what you can to head them off

in the door. Finally, keep the above-mentioned challenges in mind so that if one or more arises, you aren't caught off guard.

Transaction Stages and Timetable

Many readers will wonder about a typical timeline for completing an acquisition in the A/E/P and environmental consulting industries. Getting your firm ready for a transaction is really a process that evolves over the life of the firm— sound business practices are best implemented from the beginning. The amount of planning that should proceed conducting a search process is different for every firm— but once you have your business in order and your goals in mind, you're ready to start looking for a deal opportunity.

A merger or acquisition transaction is a complex process which is best understood when viewed as a series of cumulative chronological steps. Transactions include the following stages:

Make Your Firm Transaction-Ready

During this preliminary stage, the parties determine the reason to engage in a transaction and the deal objectives. Each party assembles its internal team and its team of outsider advisors. The seller prepares an offering memorandum to be used in the marketing effort. More importantly, each party develops a profile of the ideal transaction party.

Chapter 2 gives an overview for buyers *and* sellers on how to get ready for a deal. Chapter 3 looks specifically at preparations for buyers, and Chapter 4 covers preparations for sellers.

The Search Process and First Meeting

Each party must choose how it will seek out a transaction mate. The search process includes identifying all potential partners, contacting such firms and holding an initial meeting with qualified, potential partners. A confidentiality agreement should be signed with each potential partner with whom information will be exchanged. Chapter 5 describes both the search process and the first meeting.

A comprehensive search process should take approximately two months to complete. This involves identifying all firms that meet your basic geographic, size, and service criteria; contacting and speaking with each of those firms to establish how closely they meet your criteria and whether they are interested in a transaction; and determining internally which of these firms you wish to pursue further.

Once you have identified the candidates you want to pursue, it generally takes about another two months or more for the parties to visit each other's offices and get a first-hand look at the operation. During the second round of meetings, office visits, and telephone conversations, you should execute a confidentiality agreement that will allow you and the candidate firm to exchange information in a "secure" environment.

Corporate and Tax Considerations

Early on in the process, the primary corporate and tax aspects of the transaction must be identified. Specifically, the nature of the transfer should be determined—will the deal be a sale of assets or a sale of stock? In addition, the parties must decide whether the transaction will be taxable, non-taxable, or partially tax-deferred. Finally, the role of employment/consulting/non-competition agreements with stockholders of the seller should be decided upon, and which stockholders, if any, will become principals of the buyer. Chapter 6 looks at the corporate and tax considerations that apply to mergers and acquisitions.

Letter of Intent

Based on your review of the hard-copy information provided by the candidate firm(s) and your assessment of what is motivating the other party to consider a deal, you should draw up a letter of intent or interest. This letter should outline how you anticipate the deal will be structured. One important caveat— everything in the letter should be based upon your due diligence of the candidate(s). Preparing and finalizing the letter of intent can take about another month or so.

The letter of intent serves as a preliminary deal term sheet. The purchase price and the terms and conditions of its payment is the primary topic addressed. The letter of intent contains several non-binding provisions which are subject to due diligence. The binding provisions include access for the buyer to the seller's records, the parties' agreement to negotiate in good faith and the fact that the public announcements are to be made only by mutual agreement of the parties. The provision most sought by the buyer is a so-called "no shop clause," which restricts the seller from negotiating with anyone but buyer for a specified period. The letter of intent is covered in Chapter 7.

Due Diligence Investigation

The due diligence investigation involves gathering all information which can be obtained about the transaction partner from any source. The inquiry requires a coordinated effort among the internal team and the group of outside advisors. In Chapter 8 you will find information about how to conduct the due diligence investigation, and what you should be trying to get out of it.

After you and the candidate firm have established that this could be a mutually beneficial deal, it's time to shake the house and see if any skeletons fall out of the closets. Your due diligence process should be comprehensive enough to find any hidden land mines, be they related to finance, operations, or human resources. A good due diligence process will involve formally interviewing the owners, staff, and clients of your transaction partner. It should focus like a laser beam on protecting your organization and verifying everything you have been led to believe about the candidate organization. A comprehensive due diligence investigation usually lasts two to three months.

The Transaction Documents

The transaction documents represent the culmination of all previous efforts from the letter of intent, the tax and corporate analysis of the transition and the results of the due diligence investigation. The deal documents supersede all previous agreements and define the rights of each party at the closing and thereafter. Chapter 9 reviews these documents which represent the final written expression of the business deal.

Closing Preparation, The Closing, and Integration

The preparation for the closing involves completing the tasks necessary to document the deal and anticipating the operational issues which must be resolved and implemented in the period immediately after the closing. Finally, the post-closing business plan must be formatted.

This is where the lawyers pretty much run the show, and as a result, the process can get really bogged down. Do yourself a favor— early on, let your attorney and tax consultant know what you are planning, and advise the candidate firm to do the same. The earlier these outside advisors are aware of and involved in the process, the easier it will be to formalize the deal. It is vital that these advisors be

Good News— Mergers Do Work

Figure 1-2

A lot of newspaper reporters seem to believe that good news isn't news. That's why you see more headlines about disasters and scandals than good luck or great achievements. Maybe that's also why for every successful merger or acquisition of A/E/P or environmental consulting firms you hear about, there are at least two horror stories of good deals gone bad. It would be a shame if these industry gossips scared too many people away from giving a reasonable look to the merger or acquisition opportunity.

Internal growth is fine, but mergers are how the big firms get bigger. Here are four stories of mergers and acquisitions that worked:

1. How the big firms get bigger. The acquisition of **Bissell & Karn** (Pleasanton, CA) by **Greiner Engineering, Inc.** (Irving, TX) was handled without intermediaries from start to finish. While 1,500-person Greiner made the approach, it turned out that Bissell & Karn had been looking for a buyer. Frank Callahan, former Greiner chairman and CEO says that the entire process took over a year from the initial conversations, but once substantive negotiations were underway it was only six months till the deal was closed.

2. How coast-to-coast office networks get formed. McLaren/Hart Environmental Engineering Corp. (Rancho Cordova, CA) was created by the July 1990 acquisition of **Hart Environmental Management Corp.** (New York, NY) by **Frederick R. McLaren Environmental Engineering, Inc.** (Sacramento, CA). McLaren had been in the process of trying to expand beyond its West Coast base, and so the purchase of Hart served as the cornerstone of a larger strategy. McLaren/Hart CFO Dan Vistica reports that there was a still larger set of interests to consider as well: McLaren had been acquired in October 1988 by **Sandoz Corporation**, the U.S. arm of the giant Swiss corporation **Sandoz, Ltd.**, in a move by Sandoz to enter the environmental business. While McLaren continued to operate as an independent subsidiary, Sandoz was instrumental in providing credit and capital and in guiding larger business decisions. When an intermediary advised McLaren of Hart's availability, Sandoz supported the merger and provided members of the negotiation team.

3. How the biggest (traditional) A/E firm in the U.S. was built. The 1988 deal that created the present-day **Ellerbe Becket, Inc.** (Minneapolis, MN) also involved an intermediary. A Washington lobbyist with ties to California's **Welton Becket Associates, Inc.**, told Minneapolis-based **Ellerbe Associates** that Welton Becket's principal owner was looking to sell out. "We spent a great deal of time wondering whether it was a good fit," says Bob Degenhardt, who is now the president and CEO of The Ellerbe Becket Company. Ellerbe had already established a presence on the West Coast with its acquisition of **SGE West**, but wanted to expand that presence faster than was possible through internal growth. In the end, the merger worked culturally as well as geographically.

4. How regional firms get stronger. Hensley Schmidt, Inc., (Chattanooga, TN) didn't even know it needed a buyer when **Piedmont Olson** (Greenville, SC) first approached to discuss an acquisition. As it turned out, though, Hensley Schmidt's Canadian parent, **SNC**, was redirecting its plans away from the U.S., and the offer came at an opportune time. What really gave the deal a push, though, was the fact that Joe Hastey, then CEO at Hensley Schmidt, had contacts at Piedmont Olson. In the end, the transaction was structured as a purchase of assets and the two organizations consolidated into one.

Don't let the doom-and-gloom people get you spooked. Instead, take a look around at the national firms, regional firms, and local firms down the street from you that have made mergers work. Some of them are probably your biggest competitors— and getting bigger all the time.

involved in *structuring* the deal and drafting the letter of intent. Either way, budget at least three months to actually close the deal.

And after the deal is closed, expect a decent amount of time to pass before the companies are completely integrated. It takes time for employees to adjust to new procedures and changes in management, for corporate cultures blend, and for logistics to get straightened around.

During the period after the closing, any uncompleted or post-closing documentation must be finalized. The primary focus in this period is the integration of the parties to meet the objectives of the deal. Finally, the level of success or failure of the transaction can be measured. These issues are all covered in Chapter 10.

Conclusion

If you are thinking— seriously or otherwise— about a merger or acquisition, you probably have a thousand questions about the nuts and bolts of an actual transaction. Getting the answers to questions *before* you enter into a deal can change your negotiation position from one of weakness to one of strength. Once you know the basics of the transaction process, the common pitfalls, and the things you can do to help ensure a merger or acquisition success, you will be well on your way to seeing a transaction through to a successful end.

As we mentioned earlier, this guide was written to give buyers and sellers some practical information on how a transaction deal is structured. Unless otherwise indicated, the information applies to the deal and therefore both buyers and sellers— we'll let you know along the way if there are particular preparations, issues, or concerns that apply to one party and not the other. Regardless of which party you are, however, we recommend that you read the entire book— knowing what the other party is planning and thinking can only help you to better understand the transaction as a whole.

This *Insider's Guide to Mergers & Acquisitions* should be considered an introduction to and overview of the complex world of mergers and acquisitions. In addition to understanding the topics presented here, it is advisable to obtain appropriate legal, financial, accounting, and insurance advice before embarking on any deal.

2 How to Make Your Firm "Transaction-Ready"

How to Make Your Firm "Transaction-Ready"

☑ *Whether you're the buyer or the seller, making your firm "transaction-ready" means developing sound business practices and operating profitably, regardless of whether or not a purchase, sale, or merger is a formal part of your firm's long-term strategic plan.*

Introduction

There are hundreds of different circumstances that may serve as catalysts to initiate a transaction. If your firm is serious about a purchase or sale and is planning accordingly, that's great— it's likely that pursuing such an objective is even spelled out in the firm's strategic plan.

Transaction possibilities, however, are not always so calculated. The "catalyst" might simply be the rapport that you have developed with another firm over time. Multi-firm collaboration on projects is more the norm than the exception in the A/E/P and environmental consulting industries. Strategic alliances, prime-sub relationships, and joint ventures can all lead to solid working relationships with other firms— relationships that will (at least informally) beg the question of a possible future consolidation. And there's always the possibility that your firm will be completely caught off guard by a transaction proposal— an intermediary such as an investment banker or business broker may approach your firm on behalf of a client, inquiring as to whether you're interested in buying or selling your firm. In this case, you will have little or no time to correct operating sins of the past— problems that could hinder or ultimately terminate an otherwise legitimate, and potentially beneficial, transaction possibility.

It's just plain common sense that, even if you don't have a formal plan to pursue a sale or merger, your firm should employ sound business practices in its day-to-day operations. Making your firm "transaction-ready" is never a bad idea, since opportunities to buy, sell, or merge aren't always planned. If your firm has been operating soundly, you will be able to take advantage of unexpected but worthwhile prospects. After all, you'd hate to have to pass up the transaction opportunity of a lifetime, just because your financial statements haven't been properly prepared, or you have some sketchy HR policies to update! And if you are seriously planning for a transaction as part of your firm's formal strategic plan, you will want to do everything you can to ensure that your firm is on the best possible footing to enter into a successful transaction negotiation.

Failing to operate with sound business practices will also make your firm an unattractive, "second choice" transaction partner. Being unprepared from the get-go can lead to serious problems later in the transaction process— negotiations may be delayed because you have to take time to deal with problems along the way, or you may spend a great deal of time and energy talking with a prospective buyer or seller, only to have them scared off by your poor planning or outdated policies.

Consider the case of the prospective seller who was unable to have its financial statements certified by an independent public accountant because statements in prior years had not been prepared properly. Even though the opportunity seemed otherwise ideal, the prospective buyer was forced to walk away from the table, since its bank would not finance a firm without certified financial statements. In a case like this, unless the problem is taken care of before the seller pursues another transaction, its transaction partners are limited to buyers who do not require assistance from an outside financing source.

Operational Issues For Buyers and Sellers

So what exactly does it mean to have "sound business practices" and to make your firm "transaction-ready"? It means that you need to make sure that your business affairs are in order *before* you pursue a purchase or sale transaction. Here are some recommendations for both buyers and sellers:

Operate Profitably

Firms that operate profitably have more bargaining power when it comes to transaction negotiations— profitable firms can be buyers or sellers. A firm that is not run profitably eventually incurs losses that threaten its independence. The firm is forced to be a seller and, from a position of weakness, to look for a buyer simply to survive. Such circumstances usually lead to a transaction where very little is paid for the goodwill or going concern value of the firm. As part of making your firm ready for a successful transaction, you need to make sure your firm is financially sound. This may require dealing with some difficult issues like resolving problems with overcapacity and down-sizing, confronting unproductive principals, and reviewing niche markets. These problems aren't always present, but if they are, they weaken your position and chances of negotiating successfully.

Establish and Sustain a Bank Relationship

It is important for your firm to sustain a relationship with a bank (and a lending officer) over time, especially if you're planning to buy another firm. For most firms, it is unlikely that a merger or acquisition can be undertaken without the help of an outside lending source. Bankers who do not know your business will likely use their own criteria to determine if your transaction is a good investment. But bankers who understand your firm's business are an invaluable asset, because they are likely to see your decision to purchase another firm as a carefully planned strategic decision, and therefore a sound investment. In addition, a banker who knows your business will be better able— and probably more willing— to tailor financing to accommodate the needs of the transaction.

Keep Complete Records

Good record keeping is not something you can do in retrospect. If it's not done right from the get-go, it is very difficult to go back and reconstruct missing pieces or incomplete information. And since records provide *historical* data on the firm, it is important that a comprehensive records retention policy be established long before you consider a merger or acquisition. Good record keeping involves two components— planning carefully what information should be documented, and making sure it gets collected. Too often keeping records is one of those tasks that, albeit important, is easy to put off when staff members have a long list of "things to do."

In any transaction, the completeness and accuracy of records allows the due diligence process to proceed faster and more smoothly. In addition, good record keeping adds certain insurances for the buyer. For example, firms with well-run human resources and personnel departments have regular documented reviews of employees, uniform job classifications, and a comprehensive benefit program, all of which generally point to fewer employee issues. These practices allow a buyer to assimilate the personnel of the seller in an orderly manner and help to ensure that such matters will likely not be problematic in the future.

Keep Administrative Policies Current

Failing to stay current with issues in the administrative arena can create a minefield of potential deal killers in a merger or acquisition. Areas such as human resources, software licensing, and labor and overtime policies have each been sources of particular concern to A/E/P and environmental firms in recent years.

Consider a firm involved in well-publicized litigation that leads to fines and penalties because of failure to license software, to classify persons correctly as employees rather than independent contractors, or to properly treat employees as hourly rather than salaried personnel. Not only is this firm unlikely to be identified as an attractive transaction partner, but any deal is unlikely to get beyond the due diligence investigation once hidden liabilities are unveiled.

Confront Unproductive Principals

Figure 2-1

Even though it may be difficult to do, confronting unproductive principals and top managers will help your firm to operate more profitably.

1. Get Owners and Top Managers Working on Jobs

The average billability for all owners needs to be at least 40%. And the smaller the firm, the higher this should probably be. For example, in a 20-person firm with two owners, the two should probably average 50% billable between them. Having billable owners and top managers is more important than many people think. They must set the pace, keep employees motivated, and stay involved with clients to create revenue and identify additional work opportunities. Not being billable drains the firm, kills morale, and isolates the owners from clients who offer repeat business.

2. Confront Owners Who Want Out and Make It Happen

There's nothing worse than having someone around who draws a significant salary but gets nothing done. This hurts morale and requires the firm to pay a lot more for the stock buy-back than it should. Firms in this situation are usually better off taking the salary and benefit dollars they're paying the lame-duck owner and using it to buy out that person's stock.

Advice to Bank On

Figure 2-2

For most A/E/P and environmental consulting firms, working with a bank is a necessary part of being involved in a merger or acquisition transaction. Very few firms can get by without some sort of financing. But too often, we go "hat-in-hand" to our bankers when opportunities present themselves. Many firms don't really consider what they should be doing ahead of time to establish a relationship with their lending institutions.

Communicate with the bank regularly so they are never surprised. Bankers absolutely *hate* uncertainty. Don't put your bank in a position where they are surprised about your strategic plans or request for financing. Give them regular reports, even if you aren't bound to do so by your loan covenants. That way, they can better understand your business and *why* you need money when you do.

View your bank as a partner, not a threat. One reason many principals don't tell their bank everything is that they are afraid of them. You shouldn't be. Instead, you should ask the bank for help. The bank may provide you with information on prospective transaction partners. They may help you collect money owed to you. They may refer clients to you. And last, but not least, they may provide you with free advice on how to approach a merger or sale opportunity.

Make friends with your banker. No doubt about it, most of the personal discretion bankers had in years past about who to lend money to, or how to do things, is gone. But being friends with your banker can't hurt. There's always a benefit to having someone with access to capital who likes you, trusts you, and wants you to succeed. But you have to take an active role in cultivating the relationship. In today's banking environment, this is no small feat— it's common to hear of companies that have had a half-dozen lending officers in an equal number of years.

Spread the money you have around. Since $100,000 is the most any one account is insured for, play it conservatively and keep your money in more than one account and at more than one bank (as long as your loan agreements allow deposits in other banks). Having multiple accounts may also help you get money fast if you ever lose your primary banking relationship unexpectedly— you'll be able to go somewhere else that already considers you a client.

Be willing to change banks. The days of a banking relationship that lasts forever are over. If you are dealing with constant turnover in lending officers and are sick of re-educating new ones (i.e., explaining to them why you have no "inventory"), if your bank wants more from you than you care to give, or if your bank makes you feel like they are doing you a favor, it may be time to go elsewhere.

Institute and Implement an Ownership Program

As an owner, if you want to be able to exit the firm and get compensated for the value you've built up during your tenure, then you need to evaluate your company's ownership program. If you don't have an ownership program, then you need to develop and institute one. If you have one, but the only owners are senior principals, you should start to sell more stock to junior principals and maybe even employees who were not previously owners. The stockholders' buy/sell agreement should be updated on a regular basis. Look carefully at how the internal buy-out price is determined, and make sure the firm's cash flow can meet the terms of the stock repurchase.

Firms that are able to remain independent and profitable have an internal ownership transition program that is feasible, and a policy of selling stock to associates on a regular basis to ensure the next generation of principals. Firms that meet these goals may be buyers or sellers; firms that don't are forced to be sellers.

Adopt a Management Succession Plan

The mere transfer of stock does not guarantee that the management reins of the firm will be smoothly passed to the next generation. If you're going to successfully transfer management responsibility between generations, you need to educate younger principals well in advance. This "education" includes exposing them to the internal functions of marketing, finance, administration, and human resources, in addition to involving them in work with external advisors and lenders. And what happens if you fail to educate the next generation of leadership and management? You risk leaving the helm of the organization in the hands of people ill-prepared to guide the firm in any strategic direction.

Know What You Want Out of a Transaction

Having sound business practices is only part of getting ready for a transaction. Before you begin to outline a plan for pursuing a transaction, it's important to formulate your goals and objectives in buying a firm or selling your firm. Goals and objectives should be a result of discussions with your partners and advisors, and should be defined enough to carry you through the entire transaction. Keeping your goals in mind throughout the process will help to keep you on track. If you forgo this kind of planning, you may find yourself entering into negotiations without a clear picture in your mind of what you hope to achieve with a merger or acquisition. In addition, you will be able to articulate your objectives when the time comes.

Consult Your Advisors and Develop a Consensus

An appropriate amount of time should be spent with internal and external advisors discussing the pros and cons of pursuing a transaction, identifying the time sensitivity (if any) of completing the negotiations, and discussing the primary business aspects of the deal. The reasons to proceed with a transaction should not only be clearly understood by your advisors, but also adopted by all owners and principals at the commencement of the process. Otherwise, later you may have to fight as many battles on the inside as you do on the outside. The likelihood that the process will stall because of internal conflict and turf battles increases significantly when there is not a broad consensus or common interest among the parties involved.

The Buy/Sell Agreement Update

Figure 2-3

If your firm is considering buying or merging with another firm, make sure the buy/sell agreements with principals of your firm are up-to-date. Otherwise, you could find yourself paying more than you planned to consummate a deal.

Buy/sell agreements were established in closely-held corporations to prevent potential problems in the disposition of stock of a departing (or deceased) stockholder. The buy/sell agreement was meant to accomplish several objectives, including:

- to provide a mechanism with which the departing owner of the estate can liquidate the ownership interest;
- to set a price or provide a mechanism for determining a price for the ownership interest; and
- to prevent an ownership interest from being sold or otherwise transferred to any party the other owners find unacceptable.

Many firms intentionally keep the value of the stock in buy/sell agreements low to create minimal impact on the firm and/or stockholders when a principal leaves. Instead of paying off departing stockholders, the firm can use its cash to finance growth. Also, by keeping the stock value relatively low, the firm helps make the stock more affordable to future stockholders.

Several buying firms have strained their short-term cash reserves by acquiring companies for cash. Firms will often offer stock as an alternative to cash, but problems can arise if their stock is undervalued in a buy/sell agreement. If the firm's buy/sell agreement is based on book value, or tax basis earnings, or some outdated approach that drastically undervalues the stock, the firm may be "giving away the farm." Since the seller expects nothing less than market value for his company, the buyer may be giving up an excessive amount of stock to compensate the seller.

The solution is to ensure that your buy/sell agreement is still relevant and that it places a reasonable value on your firm's stock. If not, you need to consider rewriting your buy/sell agreement and establishing a transition plan to reflect those changes.

Be Able to Articulate Your Goals and Objectives

At the outset of negotiations, the buyer and seller have the mutual responsibility of communicating their reasons for initiating a transaction. In addition, each party must be ready and able to articulate these reasons to both employees and clients at the appropriate time. These important motivational issues should be constantly revisited during the process to remind the party of its objectives and to serve as a strategic mission statement during the transaction. This internal and external communication is very important, and is something that should be planned ahead of time.

Keep Your Initial Objectives in Mind

A search process may yield one or more firms that do not meet your original criteria, but do provide opportunities through other markets and services. In these situations, you have to remember your initial objectives in undertaking the process, and recognize that these firms represent "mission creep." Your first priority should be to focus on those firms that meet your original criteria.

Conclusion

In the world of mergers and acquisitions, having options is the name of the game when it comes to positioning your firm for a successful transaction. The qualities that may make your firm an attractive acquisition target may also establish your firm as a potential buyer. Firms that are well-managed, competitive in the marketplace, attractive to professionals seeking employment, advised by seasoned professionals, and guided by visionary leadership, will not only attract the unsolicited attention of firms looking to buy, but will also be suited to step up to the plate as buyers. In either case, your chances of seeing a transaction through to a successful end (meaning the papers get signed *and* you accomplish your transaction objectives) are significantly increased by having sound operations that put you in the strategic position of entering a transaction as either the buyer or the seller.

The next two chapters will give you more advice on how to prepare for a transaction, including determining your firm's value, assembling your group of internal and external advisors, and deciding exactly what you're looking for in a transaction partner. Chapter 3 addresses preparations from the buyer's point of view, and Chapter 4 presents them from the seller's point of view— but don't be fooled by the titles. Regardless of which party you plan to be in a transaction, you shouldn't skip the chapter for buyers if you're a seller, or the chapter for sellers if you're a buyer, because both chapters cover not only how, but *why* firms buy and sell. And the more you know about the party on the other side of the deal, the better prepared you will be to understand where they're coming from and what they're expecting.

3 For Buyers

Chapter 3

Planning to Buy a Firm?

☑ *In addition to the general operational issues that apply to both buyers and sellers, it is important to understand why firms buy other firms, as well as the particular preparations you need to make if you're planning to buy another firm.*

Introduction

Now that we've covered the general operational issues that are common to both buyers and sellers, let's take a look at the issues that are particularly important to buyers. If you're a seller, however, don't go away— you'll be especially interested in the section that outlines the different reasons why firms decide to buy other firms as you begin to think about what you're looking for in a potential buyer. In addition, it is helpful for buyers and sellers to understand not only each other's motivations, but the tasks each will be undertaking before initiating a transaction.

Why Firms Buy

What are the circumstances that might motivate a firm to look to acquire another firm? As a means of expanding and meeting strategic goals, it is often faster and less expensive to participate in a merger or acquisition to promote internal growth, open a new office, or recruit new talent. As a buyer, knowing exactly what you're trying to achieve by acquiring another firm helps you to establish clear objectives that will guide your team of internal and external advisors through the transaction process.

New Synergies in Operations

Acquiring a firm with different technical capabilities can provide the work force and diversity that allow the buyer to reach a larger critical mass and take advantage of synergies in operations. This scenario is very common in the A/E/P and environmental consulting industries. For example, an engineering firm might acquire an architectural firm to increase profits and marketing capabilities. Or, an engineering firm may purchase an environmental consulting firm which serves the same client type; instead of subbing out environmental services, the engineering firm would be able to manage both services in-house, monitor the quality of the environmental services more closely, and eliminate redundancies in overhead between the firms.

Increased Geographic Presence

Sometimes firms look to buy in order to strengthen their presence in a particular geographical area. This is especially common when the buying firm has had limited success in setting up satellite offices with a small permanent staff. Firms are turning to acquisitions because they know that starting an office from scratch— whether it's a "cold start" branch office or a completely new service— can often be more difficult and more expensive than acquiring a firm in the desired area.

Their strategic thinking rightly turns to building up the critical mass at that office to compete more effectively in the target marketplace— and there's no better way to establish yourself in the geographic market than to buy a firm already has a good reputation and client base in the area.

Expanded Areas of Expertise and Experience

Sometimes firms buy other firms in order to expand, diversify, or strengthen the buyer's areas of professional expertise and experience. A/E/P and environmental consulting firms face ever-increasing competition on all fronts, especially as consolidation trends continue to increase. A buyer may attempt to establish itself as a full-service firm by adding new disciplines, or may simply increase it's depth and project expertise enough to be able to take on larger projects.

Greater Career Opportunities

Sometimes buying another firm will prompt the growth necessary to provide career opportunities for the younger, middle management staff of the buying firm. A firm with a young senior management team may not be able to offer a career path for junior staff, particularly if the firm is not growing. An acquisition, however, can enable the growth that creates such opportunities for younger employees.

Preparing to Buy a Firm

In addition to being "transaction-ready," there are a number of considerations that are particularly important for buyers to take up before entering into any discussions with firms interested in selling. Figuring out what financial impact an acquisition might have on the firm, assembling a team of internal and experienced external advisors, and determining the qualities of an ideal transaction partner should all precede contacting potential sellers.

Evaluate Your Firm's Financial Position

Just as the seller conducts a valuation of itself, the buyer should do the same. As the buyer, it is important for you to look at your firm's revenue trends, the strength of your balance sheet, and your operating margins and profitability. What impact would the acquisition have on these financial parameters? Oftentimes financial information will reveal trends that confirm or refute whether a merger or acquisition is appropriately timed.

It is also important to investigate whether or not certain costs such as professional liability insurance and group benefits will increase or decrease for the combined entity. Other considerations include determining whether overhead expenses such as rent and general administration will decrease as a percentage of revenues, identifying deal synergies which will counter any primary financial plateaus, and reviewing the availability of stock to be offered to the seller's principals.

As the buyer, consider whether your firm has a good internal ownership transition program and stockholders' agreement in place, and whether or not these would be appealing to the principals of the seller being offered stock and ownership. Is your firm's culture one that would welcome growth and new players, or are there territorial issues that must first be resolved? You may need to honestly

The Hillier Formula

Figure 3-1

Bob Hillier has a unique— and quick— way of determining what a design firm is worth. And while his method is somewhat unusual, it makes sense in cases where firms need to sell fast.

Hillier, an architect and president of 300-person A/E firm **The Hillier Group** (Princeton, NJ), has acquired several architecture and engineering firms over the last few years, including **The Eggers Group** (New York, NY) and **GSGSB** (Clarks Summit, PA). Some of these have been firms on the brink of failure.

Hillier's unique valuation method is as follows:

- **Backlog:** It costs Hillier's firm 5% of revenues to do marketing, so any work the seller has is worth 5% of the contract value.
- **Receivables:** Give them to the seller. They're just funny money when a firm is in trouble.
- **Fixed assets:** These are only worth fire-sale prices. Pay ten cents on the dollar.
- **Key staff:** Hillier figures he'd have paid a headhunter's fee to acquire these people. Credit the seller 25-30% of the base salary on key staff.

Hillier says these numbers totaled together give him a good starting point for a sale price. He also takes into account the fact that the acquisition will provide jobs and paychecks for the otherwise soon-to-be-unemployed sellers.

We're not suggesting you try this at home, but Hillier's approach shows you what a fire sale is really all about.

address the possibility that the buyer's principals and senior associates may feel threatened by the arrival of senior principals of the seller.

Assemble an Internal Team

The buyer's internal team must also be identified and brought together. Usually the team is led by the president, CEO, or some other strategic thinker who can see the big picture for the firm. This point person is usually responsible for enacting the firm's business plan, and he or she may enlist a key financial person (and possibly the head of operations) to join in conducting the search and the initial negotiations.

The buyer does not need to be as concerned as the seller about keeping plans for an acquisition under wraps, but there are a few potential downsides to publicizing that you are in the market to buy a firm. First, if you let people know you are considering a transaction and it falls through, there may be an internal and/or external perception that the management team has somehow failed. In addition, firms who know you're a potential buyer and are interested in selling may call, resulting in a situation where your management team is tied up responding to opportunities that don't meet the your strategic goals for a transaction.

There's also the chance, especially in small, close-knit industries like A/E/P and environmental consulting, that firms may feel insulted or rebuffed should you decline to talk with them. In terms of client interaction, clients who know of your desire to acquire a firm may be concerned that you are preoccupied with transaction issues and not focused on service. How do you avoid these difficult perceptions? Be prudent about how you inform people around you— both internally and externally— of merger and acquisition plans. And always be considerate of the confidentiality issues the seller faces. There's no faster way to kill a deal than to announce your plans before the selling party is ready!

Assemble an External Team

Once the internal team is in place, buyers need to review their team of outside advisors. Buyers typically have five primary advisors: an attorney, an accountant, a financial advisor, a professional liability insurance agent, and a lending source. Before pursuing a transaction opportunity, buyers should make sure that each of these advisors is able to successfully guide the firm through a transaction. If, in reviewing your external advisors, you find that you have outgrown their expertise, are not getting responsive service, or are not billed fairly, seriously consider changing advisors. Having access to good outside advice is critical during the negotiations— there are enough potential deal-breakers in any transaction without having to worry about breaking in a new advisor halfway through the process. Be certain that your advisors are well known in the A/E/P or environmental consulting industry and that they are well versed on issues facing the profession.

There are a number of reasons why the lawyer, accountant or insurance professional you began with may not now be the appropriate advisor to see you successfully through a purchase transaction. Perhaps you've outgrown their services or are expanding in a direction that is outside of their expertise. You shouldn't hesitate to make a change if you find it necessary or in the best interest of negotiating a successful transaction. Remember that the more you prepare for a transaction, the easier and more time-efficient the process will be.

If you haven't already done so, you should also evaluate each advisor's experience. Don't be afraid to interview several advisors and ask explicit questions about the number and size of transactions they have assisted in, the types of businesses they have helped to buy or sell, whether the transactions were stock or asset sales, and what resources they have available for specific expertise support (such as pension matters, employment law, or trademarks in the case of a lawyer). It is also important to find out exactly who will be working on the transaction and to clearly note the role, fee structure, and references of each person. And if you're faced with a decision between two professionals who otherwise appear comparable, always choose the firm with specific experience in the architectural and engineering professions.

For example, an accountant experienced in the A/E/P and environmental consulting industries will likely be conversant with overhead rates, cost accounting concepts, significant financial ratios and percentage of completion for ongoing contracts. An M&A attorney with experience in the industry will understand and be skilled in discussing professional liability issues as well as the selling principal's psychological issues. A financial advisor who knows the profession will be able to discuss valuation formulas applicable to the specific practice area. The seasoned advisor will already be in tune with issues that will help you to identify likely sellers, even if it's something as basic as knowing the difference between and among architectural, engineering, interior design, geotechnical, and environmental consulting firms and their disciplines.

- ***M&A Attorney.*** Prior to the transaction, the M&A attorney's advisory role may be limited, although it becomes increasingly important as the transaction proceeds. Legal fees are generally based on an hourly rate depending on the experience of the attorney (whether he or she is a partner or an associate) or paralegal performing a task. To avoid getting an unexpected and unpleasantly large bill when the project is completed, always ask the hourly rates of the attorney who will work on the project, get an estimate of the expected fee based on previous transactions, and make certain that monthly statements are forwarded to you so you can monitor the time charges accrued. Having a written engagement letter can insure that no unpleasantly large fee surprises lurk in the transaction shadows. If your firm is not a regular client of the attorney, a retainer to be applied against actual time charges may also be required. Generally, the cost for legal services can range from a few thousand dollars to tens of thousands of dollars, depending on the scope of the transaction.

- ***Accountant.*** The buyer's accountant should counsel the buyer on the firm's financial readiness to acquire another firm, in addition to determining the tax and accounting consequences of such a transaction. The accountant can also alert the buyer of any financial issues that are out of the ordinary, and provide insight into the financial history and future projections of the business. Although accountants generally bill by the hour, in certain instances they may agree to a fixed fee arrangement for a particular project. Regardless of the arrangement, the terms for the accountant's services should also be established in writing. In most circumstances, these fees will be substantially less than those of the advising attorney.

- ***Management Consultant or Investment Banker.*** It's the job of the management consultant or investment banker to evaluate the firm's financial position, perform due diligence on the buyer's business, identify potential sellers, prepare a transaction plan to achieve the objectives of buyer, and assist in the negotiation of the business terms of the deal. The consultant or financial advisor plays the most prominent role in the process from the planning stage through the time the deal is structured. Investment bankers and management consultants sometimes work on a formula that is based on the total sales price, and usually incorporates the aggregate gross purchase price for assets or stock, non-competition payments, and consulting payments. This method of contingency fee calculation, however, can lead to charges which are outrageously high and do not correlate to the time expended or value added by the advisor. You are better off finding a firm that will undertake the engagement on an hourly basis or for a fixed fee—these firms will usually have more cost-effective billing rates, and are more likely to have an interest in finding a deal that is right for your firm, instead of one that maximizes the advisor's commission.

Form For Buyers: Deciding What You're Looking For in a Seller

Figure 3-2

Before you can initiate discussions with any firm, you need to decide what you are looking for in a seller. This form will help you focus your search on firms that match your criteria.

Buyer's Transaction Objectives:

1. ____________________

2. ____________________

3. ____________________

4. ____________________

5. ____________________

Seller's Total Staff Size: Between ________ and ________ employees

Number of Offices Desired: Between ________ and ________ offices
☐ HQ w/branch offices
☐ HQ w/o branch offices
☐ Branch office only

Buyer's Geographic Interest(s): ____________________

Seller's Firm Size: Total Staff Size: ________ Annual Net Service Revenues: $ ____________

Desired Services/Disciplines: ____________________

Other Desired Assets and Resources: ____________________

Characteristics of Seller's Client Base: ______% public ______% private ______not WBE/MBE/DBE

Involvement of Seller's Owners: Stay involved? ☐ YES ☐ NO

If YES, in what capacity? ____________________

And for how long? ____________________

Other considerations: ____________________

____

____

- ***Professional Liability Insurance Consultant.*** One of the biggest mistakes that people make in merger and acquisition transactions is not involving an insurance agent or insurance consultant until the final steps in the transaction. The insurance consultant should be brought into the process as soon as the parties are ready to move onto the letter of intent and should be an integral part of the discussions from there to the end. He or she should focus on the existing professional liability claims, the possible claims which could arise for work performed by the seller previous to the closing of the transaction, coverage for the work which is in process and which is being transferred to buyer, and finally, coverage for work and services that will be performed after the transaction.

- ***Lender or Financing Source.*** In addition to its other advisors, the buyer must select its lender or financing source and make arrangements for the necessary increase in its existing borrowings. The buyer's financing source evaluates the buyer (and later in the negotiations, the seller) to determine the type and amount of financing it will make available to buyer. At this point, it is extremely helpful to be able to capitalize on an existing relationship with a lending source, as you will be better able to argue the strategic importance of the transaction. Early on, buyers should also explore the bank's willingness to increase their line of credit for working capital or offer a term loan to purchase fixed assets.

Profiling the Ideal Seller

Finally, prior to initiating any discussions, buyers need to identify the criteria that a target firm must posses in order to be considered a potential transaction partner. In other words, as a buyer, what are you looking for in a seller? The desired traits are determined to some extent by the buyer's objectives in entering into a transaction in the first place. Is the buyer looking to create synergies in operations or increase geographic presence? The more precisely a firm can express its goals, the more focused the search for a suitable transaction partner will be—time won't be wasted meeting with firms who will not fulfill the buyer's objectives.

As a buyer outlining the search criteria for identifying a potential seller, you need to specify what you're looking for in terms of management and staff strength, areas of expertise, size, and location. In addition, you may also want to specify your price range. Figure 3-2 provides a sample worksheet that firms looking to buy can use to establish the criteria they are looking for in a seller.

Conclusion

The time and energy you invest in reviewing and planning to buy another firm are definitely resources well spent. The goal of putting work into the deal before the deal materializes is to place your firm on the best possible footing to enter into negotiations that will achieve your transaction objectives. Before you plunge head-first into an acquisition that seems like a golden opportunity, take a step back and review your own position and your strategic plans. Don't get involved in a purchase transaction unless your firm is well positioned, and the move makes good strategic business sense, because nobody benefits from a failed transaction. Every bit of effort put forth at this point— before pursuing a particular transaction opportunity— will save you valuable time and energy later on in the process.

Once you have made sure that your firm is operating profitably, that you have clear objectives in pursuing a transaction, and that you know what kind of firm you are looking to buy, it's time to conduct a search for a transaction partner. But before moving on to Chapter 5 (which looks at what is involved in initiating a transaction, from the search to contacting interested parties, to exchanging preliminary information), buyers should take a few minutes and read Chapter 4 to better understand why owners sell their firms, and what the seller will be doing to prepare for a transaction.

Sellers, if you're still with us, you now have a better idea of where the well-prepared buyer will be coming from, and the next chapter looks at the things you should focus on if you're preparing to sell your firm.

4 For Sellers

Planning to Sell Your Firm?

☑ *There are a number of reasons why firms may be motivated to sell— it's important for both buyers and sellers to understand these reasons, in addition to addressing the particular preparations a firm needs to make if the owners are planning to sell.*

Introduction

This chapter covers the issues and preparations that are particularly important to firms that are planning to sell. If you're a buyer, however, we recommend that you stay tuned, especially for the section on why firms sell— a seller's motivation can be valuable insight into whether their objectives in selling and your objectives in buying are compatible. In addition, buyers that understand how a seller has been planning enter the transaction that much farther ahead.

Why Firms Sell

So what are the circumstances that might prompt a firm to decide that it is ready to sell? Perhaps an acquisition is a means of ownership transition for the selling party, or maybe the seller sees the transaction as a means of attaining additional working capital. Alternatively, the transaction may be intended to accommodate the departure of a key principal or owner. Each scenario presents a new set of questions and considerations for the buyer to bring to the bargaining table.

Ownership Transition Failure

Sometimes firms face the prospect of not having a cash flow that is adequate enough to be able to compensate senior partners upon their retirement. With the squeeze on profitability, capital requirements brought on by advances in technology like computerization, and younger principals being reluctant or incapable of contributing capital to the firm, there may be no viable plan other than a sale or merger to finance operations and redeem senior owners. When compared with other means of ownership transition, an outside sale may yield the greatest value to owners who wish to retire when no internal transition is feasible.

Other firms may have adopted ESOPs in earlier years at high stock values and cannot service the debt associated with the leveraged ESOP. The only viable way to meet their commitments and continue to successfully manage the company is through a merger or acquisition.

Sometimes firms are forced to sell due to a lack of planning, and a sale can be the only alternative if the owner(s) wait too long to pursue an exit strategy. When speaking with principals of firms that are potentially looking to sell, it is amazing how many say, "No, we haven't really discussed ownership transition." Many of these owners are in their sixties, want to retire soon, and haven't even identified the next generation of principals. In this instance, it is less a matter of *wanting* to sell and more a matter of *having* to sell if the firm is to survive as a going concern.

Plan Ahead Figure 4-1

It's a mistake to wait until you're 60 or 65 years old to begin planning to sell your firm and retire. Zweig White & Associates often gets requests for information about selling from firms whose sole (or majority) stockholder is planning to retire the next year. With only one year of preparation, your negotiation position is weakened because buyers know you're in a hurry to sell, and that you're not willing to stick around after the deal— most buyers are looking for an ownership transition period of *at least three years*, in order to ensure a smooth transition and continued interaction with the seller's clients. When you're rushed to sell, it's almost a guarantee that you won't be able to cash in on the full value of your firm.

Principals who consider selling their firm as an option for ownership transfer should keep the following points in mind:

- Sole owners or majority stockholders should begin selling small, minority shares to the key staff 5-10 years prior to selling the entire firm. This will reward those stockholders for their work along the way *and* when the firm sells. This will also insure continuity of management and staff— a key for any buyer.
- Principals should develop a five-year (or preferably 10-year) strategic plan that incorporates a strategic sale of the firm and their plan for retirement.
- The firm should maintain a solid profitability performance over at least the three years preceding a sale— it's always easier to sell a profitable firm than one that shows consecutive losses.
- Senior management should groom a strong second-tier management team that can run the operations without the constant monitoring of the owner(s).

Once the buyer realizes that the seller's alternatives are limited by wanting to "get out quick," the seller's leverage to negotiate a deal that maximizes the price is significantly diminished.

If the primary owner of a firm dies without an internal ownership transition program, selling the firm to the existing management team over time could be the only viable alternative for the estate, other than orderly liquidation. And if the existing management team is not inclined to purchase ownership of the firm, the estate may be willing to sell the firm to the highest bidder, even if the buyer is halfway across the country.

Turnaround Situations and Rescue Missions

When one or more principals is unproductive, fails to provide a vision for the future, produces poor strategic plans, or adopts non-businesslike practices, the whole firm suffers. Sometimes the only way to untangle such issues is in the context of a merger or acquisition. Giving the firm a new start or a new identity could be the shot in the arm needed to turn the situation into a real opportunity for success.

There are a number of firms that have successfully acquired more than one financially troubled company. These firms figure that if they can help the owners and managers to turn things around, the selling firm will have an allegiance to the parent firm. Many of these so-called "rescue missions" require very little cash—the upside for potential is high, but the risk is low.

Liquidity and Future Growth

Small and mid-sized firms are those most frequently looking to sell. One recurring theme among these firms is the desire or need to grow. Many have excellent technical capabilities and an outstanding reputation, but are lacking the staff and the financial wherewithal to land large projects.

Of the approximately 69,000 firms in the A/E/P and environmental consulting industries, fewer than 100 firms have over 1000 employees, and fewer than 600 firms have more than 100 employees. If you do the math, that means that the remaining 68,300 firms (that's over 98%!) each employ fewer than 100 people. In this highly fragmented industry, a sale to a larger firm may serve to fuel working capital needs and growth that otherwise comes slowly to small firms— firms which may otherwise find themselves in a stalemate, because they can't grow until they spend more money and won't have money to spend until they grow.

War Story: The Price of Poor Planning Figure 4-2

WHEN THE OWNER of a firm dies without an ownership transition plan in place and without an agreement to sell to a third party, it is easy to see the price that might have to be paid for poor planning.

When the owner of a 28-person architectural firm in the Southeast died unexpectedly, the owner's estate was faced with either the prospect of a sale to the management team or liquidation, since no outside buyer could be promptly identified. After choosing to sell the operation to the management team, the estate discovered that the staff did not have access to capital to purchase the firm for cash. The estate was forced to finance the sale over time through the cash flow of the business.

Similarly, when a 19-person geotechnical firm in the Northeast lost its sole owner to cancer, there was no transition plan in place, but in this case, the management team did not choose to seek to purchase the firm upon the owner's death. Rather, in a hurried transaction, a third party headquartered over 3,000 miles away purchased the assets, assumed leases and contracts, and hired the employees of the seller— the buyer did not pay for goodwill and got a bargain, and the owner's estate recovered very little of his investment in the business, except for collection of receivables.

So what's the moral of these stories? Plan now before it's too late— you never know when your firm may be force to sell, and without a plan in place, you're likely to lose a great deal.

One or More Principals Leave the Firm

A firm may also look to sell when one or more of the principals decides to jump ship; otherwise, in order for the firm to continue, the remaining principals are forced to buy out the departing principal. In this circumstance, a sale serves to fund the buyout, to keep the firm running, and to preserve the core goodwill of the business.

Inactive Owner Decides To Sell

When a firm's ownership belongs primarily to an outside investor or group of investors, the investor may conclude that passive ownership has not proven a profitable investment. As a result, a transaction can be born out of the desire to create a more active ownership presence by selling the firm to the management team.

Marketing Strategy

Often a merger or acquisition can instantly broaden a firm's marketing reach. While many smaller firms looking to sell have an excellent reputation with their clients, they may not be well known beyond their existing client base. Smaller firms are often unable to devote the manpower or finances to a comprehensive marketing department. Many firms don't even have a basic marketing plan— instead they rely on repeat business, word-of-mouth, and if things aren't going well, cold or warm calls. Selling to a larger firm gives your firm the benefit of an established marketing department, as well as additional client contacts.

Other Strategic Reasons

Medium-size firms usually allow principals to engage in hands-on assistance with projects more often than they could in large firms with greater resources and a more extensive talent pool. Owners of large firms are typically more concerned about competing against other large firms (including international firms) in certain disciplines or geographic areas where they may be weak.

The consolidation being seen in the A/E/P and environmental consulting industries is similar to the consolidation phenomenon occurring in other professional service areas such as law, accounting, consulting, financial services, and advertising. The perception that there is strength in size, and that diversification of expertise can be successfully cross-marketed to a broader client base— these perceptions make firms seek out means of quickly achieving their objectives to grow and diversify. While mergers and acquisitions are not always the best course of action for meeting these goals, they are often the fastest way to capitalize on synergies of size, stabilize volatile revenues, and maximize the firm's depth of talent.

Preparing to Sell Your Firm

Along with making sure that your firm is "transaction-ready" in terms of general operations, there are a few additional things that sellers should do before approaching prospective buyers. Figuring out what your firm is worth, getting your internal and external advisors on board, and outlining criteria for target buyers are all important steps that will make transaction go more smoothly once it is initiated.

Determine a Realistic Range of Value for Your Firm

The seller should thoroughly review the firm's financial position in anticipation of a transaction. Make sure that financial statements are adjusted to exclude items such as personal expenses and loans to stockholders. Review the status and quality of accounts receivable, work in progress and backlog, and address any problems. You should also determine the market value (as opposed to book value) of the assets, and analyze the potential range of value of your intangibles. Your firm may also want to think about hiring an outside firm to prepare a valuation for your internal use during the negotiations.

The seller's valuation will allow its principals to identify a range of realistic value for the firm and anticipate how a particular buyer may view the seller's strengths and weaknesses. This helps to head off the possibility of a seller going into a negotiation with a highly inflated, false sense of value, which is the most common

Don't Judge "Book Value" By the Cover Figure 4-3

How important is "book value" to the people making acquisitions of A/E/P and environmental consulting firms? Too important to some of them, based on Zweig White & Associates' experience.

"Book value" is the bottom line of a design or environmental consulting firm's balance sheet— total assets minus total liabilities. It's also referred to as "owners' equity," "stockholders' equity," or "net worth."

Because the book value number usually comes from an independent accountant who follows generally accepted accounting principles, many buyers and sellers treat it like the gospel. Or at least, they believe it's the only "hard" number to go on when determining value. Plus it's readily available for almost any firm.

However, in reality, not only is book value not as "hard" a number as some people think, it has nothing to do with the value of the business as a going concern. For one thing, accounting rules on depreciation produce fixed asset numbers that may have little relation to the actual replacement cost or fair market value of equipment; and the numbers for work in progress, accounts receivable, and other assets may also need significant downward adjustments from what appears in financial statements. Perhaps most importantly though, professional services firms aren't really asset-intensive businesses anyway. Their value lies in the potential for future growth in revenue and profit streams. Or in their strategic importance to a particular buyer or type of buyer.

Bob Perry, executive VP of 5,300-employee environmental giant **Dames & Moore** (Los Angeles, CA), has an interesting approach to book value. When looking at an acquisition, Perry looks at revenues and profitability, then considers what kind of working capital will actually be necessary to operate the firm as planned. If the equity in the firm is less than this amount (as is often the case with a growing business), the price is adjusted downwards. If equity exceeds working capital needs (the case with many stable, mature businesses), then the excess increases the price paid to the seller.

War Story: The Low-Ball Offer

Figure 4-4

LOW-BALL offers are generally a negotiation *faux pas*. Low-balling sometimes works, but you risk annoying the seller and jeopardizing a deal with real potential— more often than not, it's as much a pride issue for the seller as it is a money issue. Wise sellers will have a number of options so that they can dismiss potential buyers who make low-ball offers and move on to firms who are serious about the worth of the seller.

Once in a while, a low-ball offer is accepted, probably because of some extenuating circumstance that is not known to both parties at the time of the offer. Buyers should be suspicious of someone who accepts a low-ball offer— does the seller know something they're not revealing?

One southern California geotechnical firm discovered the dangers of low-balling the hard way. They had identified a small materials testing firm in Arizona, and after a few meetings, really hit it off with the owners. The California firm jokingly made a low-ball offer and was shocked when their offer was accepted. Little did they know, however that the Arizona firm had several pending lawsuits, and the owners were looking to be rescued.

The moral of the story? Never make a binding low-ball offer without conducting thorough due diligence, because the firm might not be all the seller claims.

non-starter in merger and acquisition discussions. This situation almost always results in a buyer who quickly cuts off the discussion, and a seller who is disappointed because its unrealistic expectations have not been met.

With each potential buyer, the seller should also assess what the buyer is looking for, and negotiate accordingly. As a seller, keep in mind that different buyers will value different aspects of your firm for different reasons. The asking price in any transaction should be a combination of both the value of the firm on paper and any intangible value your firm may have to that particular buyer. And beware of the buyer who low-balls— if you smell a low-baller, stick to your guns and to your asking price. A wise financial negotiator will anticipate the arguments of the buyer and formulate good counter-arguments in order to get the best deal possible out of the sale.

Assemble an Internal Team

The seller needs one internal group to serve as its transaction negotiating team and another to oversee the integration process. The seller's internal team is typically made up of the controlling stockholders or an individual leader charged with negotiating the sale and representing the interests of the firm. This individual is responsible for conducting the search for a buyer, and overseeing the initial negotiations. Once a high-interest, high-fit firm has been identified, other key senior people from the firm may be added to the team.

The negotiating group should be composed of only a few senior members of the firm— if fact, the fewer the better (although enough to get the job done), since the fact that the firm is for sale must be held in the strictest confidence to prevent interrupting the seller's operations. Another reason to keep things quiet is that, once they're "in the know," the seller's competitors may use the information to hire away employees or to win jobs. Accounts receivable become much harder to collect when the word of a possible sale gets out. Additionally, clients may become concerned by the news that you are looking to sell. For all of these reasons, the internal group should take all necessary precautions to keep files secure and keep the initial negotiations confidential. If possible, don't communicate by the office fax if possible. Hold all planning and negotiation meetings outside the office. Have any materials sent to you via mail marked personal and confidential. Do everything possible to avoid any suspicion.

When and how information about the transaction should be revealed to the clients of the seller is often a very sensitive issue. Clearly you do not want rumors to reach clients before you have the chance to inform and reassure them yourself. The buyer, however, may want to approach the seller's clients at some point to determine if they will perceive the buyer favorably. One intelligent way for the buyers to deal with this issue is to hire an independent third party to interview the seller's clients under the pretext of a client satisfaction survey. The appropriate point in the negotiations to break the news to clients is different for every transaction— just be sure to keep close tabs on all information and stay one step ahead of the word on the street.

There are a few cases where you may have to disclose your transaction plans to clients earlier than you would like, however. For example, in asset sale transactions, contract assignment approval may be required from clients before those contracts can be assumed by the buyer. It is still important to contact clients in a controlled manner that allows you to allay their fears right from the beginning.

Assemble an External Team

In addition to its internal team, the seller needs to assemble a team of outside advisors. Sellers usually have four primary advisors: an attorney, an accountant, a management consultant or business broker, and a professional liability insurance consultant. Before pursuing a transaction opportunity, sellers should review each of their advisors to make sure that they are qualified to lead the firm through a successful sale. It is especially important that sellers have good outside advice during the transaction process to insure that they are not taken advantage of by an opportunistic buyer. All external advisors should also be in tune with the issues particular to the A/E/P and environmental consulting industries.

Be aware of the possibility that your current lawyer, accountant, or insurance professional may not be the appropriate advisor to see you successfully through a sale transaction. If you've outgrown their services or have expanded beyond their expertise, don't hesitate to make changes that are in the best interest of negotiating a successful transaction. Having a good external advising team further insures that a seller will be able to negotiate from a secure position.

If you decide to make a change, screen your current or potential advisors to be sure that they have the skills and experience necessary to guide you successfully through a transaction. Also take a close look at whether your advisors are objective or whether they might actually have a disincentive should your firm be sold— after all, the advisor may lose a valuable business client!

You should question all of your advisors or potential advisors about their past transaction experience, including the types of businesses they have helped to sell and whether the transactions were stock or asset deals. It may also be useful to compare the resources that different advisors have available for specific expertise support (on pension matters or employment law, for example). In addition to determining each advisor's qualifications, find out exactly who will be working on your transaction and note the role, fee structure, and references for each person.

If you're faced with a decision between two professionals who otherwise appear comparable, always choose the advisor with specific experience in architectural and engineering professions. For example, if your accountant is familiar with issues in the A/E/P and environmental consulting industries, you will be more appropriately advised on issues like overhead rates, cost accounting concepts, and percentage of completion for ongoing contracts. Your financial advisor will be able to select a valuation formula that is appropriate for your firm if he or she is familiar with your profession. And advisors who know the difference between and among architectural, engineering, interior design, geotechnical, and environmental consulting firms and their disciplines can make all the difference when it comes to finding a likely buyer and carrying out a win-win negotiation.

- ***M&A Attorney.*** The role of your M&A attorney will likely be limited prior to negotiating a transaction. Once discussions have started, however, their role increases significantly. Legal fees will most likely be based on an hourly rate, and are calculated according to the experience of the attorney (depending on whether he or she is a partner or an associate) or paralegal performing a task. You can prevent unexpected and unpleasantly large bills by getting some information in advance— namely an outline of the hourly rates of anyone who will work on the project and a fee estimate based on previous transactions.

  The time charges that are accrued each month should be closely monitored, and you may even want to have the rates and other charges outlined in a written form prior to engaging the services of an attorney. The attorney will probably require a retainer to be applied against actual time charges if your firm is not a regular client. Depending on the scope of the transaction, you should expect to budget anywhere from a few thousand dollars to tens of thousands of dollars for the cost of legal services.

- ***Accountant.*** The seller's accountant advises the seller on the tax and accounting consequences of a possible transaction, provides insight into the financial history and future projections of the business, and informs the seller of any unusual financial issues. The accountant can forecast the gross proceeds and net after tax proceeds each stockholder will receive based on various sales prices and types of transactions (sale of assets, sale of stock, taxable transaction, nontaxable transaction). Although accounting fees are usually calculated on an hourly basis, in certain instances services may be performed for a fixed fee. Whatever the arrangement, make sure the terms of the engagement are fully understood and established in writing. These fees should be substantially less than those of the advising attorney.

- ***Management Consultant or Financial Advisor.*** It's the job of the management consultant, investment banker, or other financial advisor to determine a realistic value for the business, identify potential buyers, prepare

War Story: Make Up Your Own Mind Figure 4-5

MAX, AN AMBITIOUS young owner of a successful engineering firm, decided he was ready for a change. He was looking to get out of the firm and relocate with his family to a different state, but would only do so if a transaction proved to be lucrative enough to give him a decent return on his investment, and facilitate the family's relocation. In an effort to find a buyer for his business, he conducted a comprehensive national search, and received three or four very attractive offers.

One of the firms offered Max top dollar for his firm, and even offered to set up a new office in the state of Max's choice. Everything looked rosy, but Max prudently requested that his accountant review the offers and give an opinion. After looking over the offer, the accountant told Max that it was pretty good, but that he would recommend holding out for something bigger and better. Max was in a dilemma. On one hand, he had received an offer that was more than he expected, and gave his family the move they wanted. On the other hand, a trusted advisor was telling him to refuse the offer, and hold out for a better opportunity— a tempting alternative.

The more Max thought about the two choices, however, the more he began to doubt the advice of his accountant. "Does my accountant have many engineering firm clients? Does he really understand my business?" Max asked himself. "Has he built a successful business? Is he more successful than I am? Other than dealing with tax issues and bookkeeping, does he know anything about running an engineering firm?" The answer to each of Max's questions was no, and with that, Max decided to trust his own instincts and accept the buyer's offer.

The accountant's advice nearly caused Max to miss a terrific opportunity— don't let this happen to you. In evaluating your own situation, be sure that you do what Max did when all of the advice is in— trust yourself to make the final decision.

and implement a marketing strategy that will achieve the objectives of seller, perform due diligence on the seller's business, prepare a sales memorandum or summary of the selling terms, and assist in the negotiation of the business terms of the deal. As noted earlier, deciding on a realistic range of value for a selling firm is a useful, preliminary step in the process. There is no need to have two separate advisors if the firm conducting the valuation also provides services in marketing and negotiating a deal.

Before the transaction, through the initiation of discussions and the structuring of the deal, the financial advisor plays the most prominent role in the process. Most investment bankers work on contingency, using a formula that is based on the total sales price. The formula usually incorporates the aggregate gross purchase price for assets or stock, non-competition payments, and consulting payments, and it can lead to fees which are outrageously high and do not reflect the time expended or value added by the banker. You should try to find a firm that will take the engagement on an hourly basis or for a fixed fee. Even though the payments are due to the advisor regardless of

Beware of Valuation Charlatans Figure 4-6

There's a lot of bad advice being given out there on how much money firms are worth. Some consultants and business brokers tell clients that their companies are worth two, three, or even more times what the firm is probably really worth.

Why do they do this? Because they're trying to get you to hire them, and their idea of how best to do that is to tell you what you *want* to hear, not what you *need* to hear. It's a classic real estate strategy. Sign up the listing at any price, then bust 'em in the chops to lower their price when the house won't sell. The bottom line is that a firm is worth what someone else will pay for it.

whether or not a transactions is consummated, this kind of arrangement eliminates the risk that a broker might to push a deal on the seller to guarantee payment, and results in a fairer (and lower) amount paid.

- *Professional Liability Insurance Consultant.* As mentioned in the previous chapter, people often make the mistake in merger and acquisition transactions of not involving an insurance agent or consultant until the transaction is in the final stages. Contrary to popular practice, the insurance consultant should be consulted as soon as the parties are ready to move to the letter of intent, and should remain an integral part of the discussions until the transaction is completed. The liability insurance specialist needs to focus on professional liability claims that already exist, claims which might arise for work done before the closing, and coverage for the work-in-progress which will be transferred to buyer. The buyer also needs to evaluate it's post-transaction insurance needs— an increased workload or new areas of service may require additional insurance.

Profiling the Ideal Buyer

Based on their transaction objectives, the seller should attempt to identify the major attributes in a buyer that suggest a good match. Sellers should consider the qualities an ideal transaction partner would possess in tandem with what their firm has to offer in a sale— knowing exactly what you are looking for will not only make the search process more efficient, but will increase the likelihood that you'll find a good match and end up striking a deal.

If the principals wish to sell for cash and plan to retire after a brief transition period, then the seller may not be too concerned about the profile of the buyer. On the other hand, if the firm is being sold for strategic reasons and the selling principals will become principals of the buyer or will receive stock for all or some of the consideration, then the size, areas of expertise, reputation, profitability, and cultural values of the buyer are much more important to the seller. In addition, if the seller's principals are looking for operating autonomy after the sale as a division or branch office, then the location of the buyer, its track record from previous acquisitions, and its operating philosophy also become important considerations. Figure 4-7 provides a sample worksheet that firms looking to sell can use to establish the criteria they are looking for in a buyer.

Once the qualities of an ideal prospect have been determined, the seller should develop a written profile of the kinds of buyers that will be targeted and ap-

Form For Sellers: Deciding What You're Looking For in a Buyer

Figure 4-7

Before you can initiate discussions with any firm, you need to decide what you're looking for in a buyer. Use this form to establish criteria that will help you focus your search.

Seller's Transaction Objectives:

1. ____________________
2. ____________________
3. ____________________
4. ____________________
5. ____________________

☐ Selling entire firm ☐ Selling branch office(s) only ☐ WBE ☐ MBE ☐ DBE

Seller's Location(s): # of employees:

HQ: ____________________, __________ __________

Office #1: ____________________, __________ __________

Office #2: ____________________, __________ __________

Office #3: ____________________, __________ __________

Annual Net Service Revenues: $__________ Total Staff Size: __________

Seller's Services/Disciplines: ____________________

Other Assets and Resources of Seller: ____________________

Seller's Client Base Characteristics: ______% public ______% private ______% not WBE/MBE/DBE

Plans of Seller's Owner(s): Stay involved? ☐ YES ☐ NO

If YES, in what capacity? ____________________

And for how long? ____________________

Requirements for Potential Buyers:

Size: __________ Location: ____________________

Firm Type/Services Offered: ____________________

Other: ____________________

War Story: Be Realistic

Figure 4-8

THE PROPRIETOR of a small environmental consulting firm approached an advisor for advice on selling. Located in the Northeast, the firm served mainly petroleum clients, and with thoughts of starting up a new business venture, the owner was interested in seeing what kind of a return he could get on his investment in the environmental consulting firm. Each time he had his firm valued, however, the value was determined to be lower than what he expected, mainly because he refused to account for the fact that the bulk of his work relied on only one client— and if that client was ever to pull out, there was no guarantee that the business would survive. And because the seller needed $4.5 million to start his next business, that's how much he wanted to make on a sale of his environmental consulting business. Holding onto his skewed sense of value, he waited several years, hoping that with time, the firm value would appreciate. Unfortunately, before he could look into another sale, the environmental consulting market collapsed, he lost all of his clients, and resorted to working out of his house. Needless to say, the seller's $4.5 million dollar hopes vanished as a direct result of his unrealistic expectations.

proached. Unless a potential buyer comes close to meeting these criteria, the principals of the seller should not consider even preliminary discussions with the transaction candidate.

Conclusion

For a seller, the goal of investing time, energy, and resources before pursing a deal is to position your firm to enter a transaction with clear objectives in mind, and to put you on a more level playing field with potential buyers. Firms that get involved in a sales transaction before they are well positioned are easy prey for opportunistic buyers, and risk a transaction that yields little or no return on the selling owner's investment. Every bit of effort put forth at this point— before pursuing a particular transaction opportunity— will save you valuable time and energy down the road.

Once your firm is operating profitably, you have clear objectives in pursuing a buyer, and you have an idea of the kind of firm you are looking to sell to, then you are ready to conduct a search for a transaction partner.

Buyers, you should now have a better idea of what a selling firm may be doing to get ready for a transaction. From this point forward, each chapter will address the transaction as a whole, including both the buyer's and the seller's point of view and responsibilities— points that are *exclusive* to either buyers or sellers will be identified when necessary.

With this in mind, let's move on to Chapter 5, which looks at what is involved in conducting a search, contacting interested parties, and exchanging preliminary information.

5 The Search Process and First Meeting

Chapter 5

The Search Process and First Meeting

☑ The search process involves identifying potential buyers or sellers, executing a confidentiality agreement, and making preliminary contact with interested parties.

Introduction

Once you've gotten your firm in order, and you know what your objectives are and what you're looking for in a transaction partner, it is time to conduct a search.

If a joint venture or successful working relationship brought you to the bargaining table, then you might be wondering why you need to conduct a search at all. Can't you just go ahead and formally approach the prospect to confirm a mutual interest in pursuing a deal? Sure you can, but is it the best option? We say no. Why? Because firms that give themselves several options are in a better position to successfully negotiate a deal. If in the course of discussions with one firm you find that there is a culture conflict or one of you is losing interest, you may want to withdraw and pursue other opportunities— opportunities you won't know about unless you've conducted a search. Giving yourself options insures that you won't be back at ground zero when negotiations with the firm you thought was "a sure thing" fall apart.

There are a number of ways you can identify interested buyers or sellers— some ways are more aggressive than others, some are more effective than others. Informal networking, blind advertisements, and formal listings are all common techniques used to locate firms that might be interested in finding out more about your opportunity. And whether you decide to conduct a search on your own or enlist the help of an intermediary, your search relies on the criteria you established in Chapter 3 if you're a buyer, or in Chapter 4 if you're a seller.

Conducting your own search requires that you choose a comprehensive search process. A great deal of time and energy is needed to throw the nets wide and then sort through the catch for the best fish. We recommend finding an experienced intermediary to conduct the search for you, based on the parameter you've set with your transaction partner criteria. Keep in mind that the more choices you have the better your chances of finding a motivated and capable transaction partner.

The search should include a screening process which is aimed at narrowing down what may initially be a long list of target firms. Along the way, it is normal for firms to lose interest or for you to decide not to pursue further discussions. When this happens, you can return to other firms identified in the initial search process. Because there may be contact with a number of firms and you will be interacting with many persons outside of your team, it is important that the search and contact process be implemented and controlled in a systematic and professional manner.

War Story: Buyers Spread the Word

Figure 5-1

RECENTLY, A RATHER SMALL firm in the Boston area was acquired by a foreign firm. The president of more than one larger competitor was heard to say that he would have been very interested in the seller and wished he had known the firm was for sale. In talking with his attorney, the attorney pointed out that the president hadn't made it generally known that his firm was interested in purchasing another firm, and the seller could not have been expected to know. By not letting the industry know that it was a potential buyer, the firm not only missed an opportunity to acquire a competitor— it now faces a stronger, well-financed competitor.

Do-It-Yourself Searches vs. Use of an Intermediary

Other than your own time (which may be substantial), do-it-yourself searches are low or no cost endeavors that are often very successful— how the search is carried out is more important than who conducts it. But unless you have a great deal of time on your hands, or have a trustworthy, experienced partner who can take on your day-to-day operational responsibilities at the firm, we recommend hiring an intermediary. And even if you have the time and resources to take the project on yourself, there are a number of added benefits to having an experienced intermediary at your side.

There are several other issues that come up as discussions continue—issues that can be difficult to handle just by yourself, like maintaining confidentiality. There are the questions of how you avoid awkwardness in commencing and terminating discussions, and whether or not you will be able to keep discussions afloat when there are differences of opinion. And how do you avoid discussing issues which are personal to one or more of the principals (like early retirement, repayment of stockholder loans, or a need to work less than full-time due to family reasons such as illness)?

Intermediaries

Working with an intermediary, such as a management consultant or investment banking firm, has great merit— it gives both buyers and sellers critical access to expertise and experience in mergers and acquisitions. Intermediaries give sellers control over their entry into the marketplace, and provide buyers with a more comprehensive search process. Introduction through a third party also creates an important link between the buyer and seller, through which many difficult issues can be filtered and resolved. In addition to conducting a search, intermediaries can often be retained to contact firms which fit the search criteria and identify likely matches among those who respond that they are interested in the opportunity. They can also arrange an initial meeting between you and the firms you have chosen to talk with, assist in deal structuring, negotiations, due diligence, valuation, and integration planning and support. It is also beneficial to have an intermediary available throughout the negotiations and closing process to help you work through potential deal-breakers that will inevitably surface.

It is important to consider the parameters of your search before engaging an intermediary. A locally-based intermediary working with a seller will most likely focus only on buyers in the immediate geographic area. An intermediary with national or international presence and experience is more likely to seek out interested and right-fit buyers based on an understanding of the basic criteria and strategy set forth by the seller.

There are two main types of organizations which serve as intermediaries— investment bankers or business brokers, and management consulting firms.

Investment Bankers and Business Brokers

Investment bankers are not interested in being involved in the mergers and acquisitions of most firms in the A/E/P and environmental consulting industries—the deals are too small. They can get higher fees for investing their resources in other industries that boast large numbers of companies with publicly traded stocks.

If you have a choice of advisors, business brokers are not ideal for businesses in our industry either. Business brokers have a deservedly poor record in assisting A/E/P and environmental consulting firms, partially because they work in a variety of unrelated industries. They generally have a wealth of local knowledge, like who's interested in selling a tavern or restaurant, but they know very little about our industry. In addition, business brokers typically work on a contingency-fee basis, and as a result may do or say anything to make a deal. Often, they draw their candidates from a limited pool, and then lose credibility because they try to "force fit" marriages.

Investment bankers and business brokers both typically specialize in certain industries (i.e., manufacturing or distributing) or types of businesses (i.e., retail or wholesale) and may not be in tune with the issues that are critical in A/E/P and environmental consulting firm deals, such as ownership by principals, cultural fit, and the need to have the consent of the owners of the seller before proceeding with serious negotiations.

Questions to Ask When Shopping for an Intermediary

Figure 5-2

Asking questions *before* you choose an intermediary will help ensure that you find someone who has both the expertise and experience necessary to see you through a successful transaction.

- Do you specialize in assisting A/E/P and environmental consulting firms?
- What other industries do you specialize in?
- Do you work locally? nationally? internationally?
- What is your process for identifying a seller? a buyer?
- Do you work on commission?
- Do you work on retainer?
- What is your fee structure?
- What is your reputation in the industry?
- Can I speak with other clients?

War Story: The Ineffectiveness of Non-Discrimination

Figure 5-3

AN ATTORNEY received a call from a reputable business intermediary who was attempting to sell a firm. The intermediary's response as to how he valued the firm was not with reference to traditional ratios applicable to the discipline of the firm. When asked who was on his marketing list, he read a list of every large firm in the geographic area, revealing that he had no understanding of whether the firm practiced in the same or complimentary areas. He had no idea of which firms might have an acquisition mentality or the financial strength to buy the seller, much less why each firm would want to enter into the transaction.

Although the intermediary had not disclosed the identity of the seller, when presidents of some of the firms of the list were later contacted, in each case, the principal was able to identify the seller with ease. Many questioned why their firm was on the marketing list. At the end of the marketing effort by the intermediary, everyone in the geographic area knew the firm was for sale—not the result the seller wanted.

A firm specializing in the architectural and engineering professions would have targeted only those firms in the geographical area that were likely to be interested in the opportunity and firms outside the area whose entry into the region would make sense from a strategic point of view.

Management Consulting Firms

Management consulting firms have the distinct advantage of maintaining a broad-based knowledge of A/E/P and environmental consulting industries, and when their information is not tied to one geographical area, they offer the added benefit of being able to perform a national or even international search. These firms also tend to know which firms may be inclined to be open to an opportunity to buy, sell, or merge, and they have the experience necessary to help see your negotiations through to a successful end. In addition to conducting acquisition searches and providing firm sale assistance, management consulting firms like Zweig White & Associates also offer a comprehensive suite of services (including deal structuring, negotiations, due diligence, valuation, and integration planning and support) to assist both buyers and sellers in planning and executing successful mergers, sales, and acquisitions.

Many firms try to find a buyer by approaching prospective sellers on a one-to-one basis to establish whether those firms have an interest in the opportunity. This approach seldom results in the best possible outcome for three reasons. First, by approaching a small number of firms, you reduce the chances of making a deal happen and depress the potential sale price. Second, by approaching firms directly, you *increase* the chances that word will leak out in an inappropriate manner to both clients and employees that you are looking to sell your operation. Finally, under this approach, some of the firms that you contact, while appearing to be interested, may actually be "tire kickers." They may just want to learn more about a specific market, or more about their competition— you. They may not

Comparison of Investment Banker and Management Consulting Firm Services

Figure 5-4

This chart will help you compare some typical characteristics of investment bankers and management consultants, and decide which is the right choice for your firm. Regardless of which one you choose, it is smart to have all services, conditions, and provisions for payment spelled out in an engagement agreement prior to the commencement of the project.

INVESTMENT BANKER	MANAGEMENT CONSULTING FIRM
General Proposal Items ■ proposal to provide investment banking services ■ investment banker will be engaged as the sole representative	**General Proposal Items** ■ proposal to provide acquisition or firm sale assistance
What Investment Bankers Will Do ■ research the firm and develop a prospectus (for sellers) ■ conduct a search for target firms ■ contact and interview interested investors ■ evaluate interested investors ■ negotiate and communicate with investors on behalf of the company until the closing or the contract period expires, whichever comes first	**What Management Consulting Firms Will Do** ■ research the firm and develop a prospectus (for sellers) ■ conduct a search for target firms ■ contact and interview interested buyers or sellers ■ evaluate interested buyers or sellers ■ *provide additional consulting services (negotiation, due diligence, etc.) as requested by the client
Provisions for Payment ■ paid a percentage of the entire purchase price in cash at the time of the closing. (The purchase price equals total consideration paid in connection with the sale. Total consideration includes: cash and non-cash consideration, such as stock, paid at the closing, the total amount of any and all balance sheet liabilities assumed by the buyer in connection with the transaction, the face amount of any other indicated future payments, secured or unsecured, and any other forms of consideration rendered at the closing, including consulting or non-competition agreements.) ■ retainer fee deductible against the fee to be paid at the closing ■ expenses (travel, copying, shipping) billed separately ■ contract period is 9 months, but the closing fee must be paid if the company is merged or acquired within 12 months of the end of the period.	**Provisions for Payment** ■ flat rate (determined by the scope of the project) ■ usually payable in installments ■ *pre-approved services outside the scope of the project paid on an hourly rate ■ no contingency or commission payment

have the clout to make the decision themselves, but instead must refer the matter to a parent company. Or, they may not place an acceptable value on your firm.

You may invest significant time and resources pursuing one of these firms, engaging in negotiations and exchanging information, only to find they have neither the will nor the wallet to consummate a deal. If this happens, you will find yourself three months down the road and back at square one. Then more deals may be explored, one at a time, and years may pass. This "water torture" method wastes time and discourages everyone involved. A management consulting firm, however, is able to conduct a comprehensive search process that identifies a number of potential sale or acquisition targets. All options can be developed and reviewed simultaneously, maximizing the buyer's or seller's possibility of making the best choice in initiating discussions.

Whether you use a consulting firm, investment banker or business broker, it is prudent for a buyer or seller to engage an intermediary according to a written agreement.

Search Techniques

Whether you have decided to hire an intermediary or conduct the search process on your own, there are a number of ways to go about identifying firms that might be interested in discussing the possibility of participating in a merger or acquisition. Three common search techniques are informal networking, blind advertisements, and formal listings. Each option has its advantages and disadvantages with regard to scope, confidentiality, expense, time efficiency, and effectiveness.

Informal Networking

Informal networking involves making a list of organizations that your firm knows through local professional associations or competitive bidding situations. Local lawyers or accountants who practice in the profession may also be good people to contact for suggestions. Although this may appear to be an "in-the-right-place-at-the-right-time" approach, mutual contacts and interests may yield a large number of firms that are good matches in terms of culture and expectations.

This method has a number of limitations, however. If your search criteria calls for a partner firm that currently practices in the same geographical area, this technique may yield several other interested firms. If you are not familiar with the geographic area you wish to expand to, then informally "getting the word out" is not only difficult, but will yield marginal results.

In addition, informal networking is a more realistic strategy for buyers than for sellers. Firms which are unable to conclude a successful internal ownership transition or which are in some financial difficulty are likely candidates to be acquired. An A/E/P or environmental consulting firm which is seeking a buyer simply cannot afford to let the word get out in an uncontrolled manner that it is for sale. Clients may lose confidence in the ability of the firm. Competitors might use this information to recruit key employees away from the seller, and prompt those who are not recruited to seek other employment— either case will significantly diminish the seller's assets. Competitors have also been known to drop this information in the bidding process for jobs. In order to stay in control of the search process and stay ahead of the word on the street, sellers are advised to avoid the informal networking search option. Informal networking yields the best results for firms looking to buy in a geographic area with which they are very familiar.

Blind Advertisements

Buyers or sellers sometimes run anonymous ads in trade publications like *ENR* and *Architectural Record.* This method allows advertisers to evaluate the firms that respond without compromising their own confidentiality.

This search method, however, has not shown itself to be particularly comprehensive or effective— you can't guarantee that the firms who see your ad are the ones you are trying to target. Advertisements simply put your message out there and you wait for someone who is interested or thinks they're a good match to inquire. In addition, many firms are unwilling to respond to an anonymous ad, because they are at the mercy of someone they can not identify— perhaps the person that placed the ad is a competitor that would benefit from knowing your firm is looking to sell. Lastly, advertisements in trade publications often carry the stigma that the firm placing the ad is desperate to find a transaction partner, therefore they should generally be used as a last resort.

Examples of Blind Advertisements

Figure 5-5

Newspapers, magazines, business journals, and trade publications often have a classified ad section where you can find firms that are looking to buy, sell, or merge. Here are some sample advertisements.

Business Opportunities

- **For Acquisition:** Well established landscape architecture/survey firm seeking investor for its $10MM volume Northwest subsidiary. Three state coverage with strong presence in Washington State. Serious and confidential inquiries only. Contact Box A.
- **Merger/Acquisition:** Privately held West Coast A/E Firm with offices in WA, OR, CA, MT, ID, WY, and NV. Available for Merger/Acquisition. Rapidly growing, established in 1978 with gross billings of $18 million in 1994 and current backlog exceeding $11 million. Would consider overseas firms. Reply to Box B.
- **Seeking Purchase:** Established southeast regional full-service consulting engineering firm with some environmental projects seeks to purchase a Texas firm with engineering strength on environmental projects. Box C.
- **Merger or Acquisition:** A/E firm with two NY offices seeks merger or acquisition by a larger firm looking to take advantage of NY's growing market. Our firm is well established and has an excellent reputation in the building and environmental markets. We are profitable and have a substantial backlog. Please send a letter of interest to: Box D.

If you do choose to use this method, it is important that you have a confidentiality agreement and some form of offering memorandum prepared to send to the prospective buyer or seller.

Formal Listings

There are a number of companies which publish lists of design professional firms that want to be acquired or are looking to acquire other firms. If you are a seller, you can place your name on the list so that potential buyers can contact you, or you can call listed buyers directly. If you are a buyer, then you can choose to contact the sellers listed, or simply include your firm as an interested buyer, and see who comes to you looking to sell.

The greatest shortcoming of the formal listing search technique is that the only firms these companies can bring to your attention are firms that are already listed with them — firms which are looking to sell are probably struggling and firms which are looking to buy are passively waiting to be contacted by a seller. This could not only take a long time, but when firms do respond, your management team may be stuck fielding calls from people who might be extremely interested, but who do not even remotely match your criteria for a buyer or seller.

The Process We Recommend

As we mentioned in the introduction, the most important characteristic of your search process is that it be comprehensive enough to yield a number of solid opportunities for you to pursue. And this applies regardless of whether you're doing the search yourself or getting help from an intermediary. Keep in mind that the success of your deal relies on the success of your search process.

The biggest problem with the techniques we listed above is that they are limited in their scope and in their effectiveness— in short, they are not comprehensive means of finding interested and capable transaction partners. After trying many combinations of techniques, we have come up with the process that we recommend be employed by every buyer, seller or intermediary.

In the sections that follow, we have divided the process into a number of steps— the process that buyers should use to identify potential sellers is given first, followed by the process that sellers should use for identifying potential buyers. The process may seem long and involved, but if you want to insure the best odds for accomplishing your purchase or sale objectives, don't waste your time on limited means of finding partners. Instead, follow the tried-and-true process outlined below— or better yet, find an intermediary who will follow it for you.

For Buyers: Identifying Potential Sellers

The goal in searching for a seller is to bring as many interested candidates as possible to the buyer's attention. In general, prospective buyers are not as concerned as sellers about keeping their identity a secret. Buyers conducting a search on their own are often in a position to contact potential sellers directly based on prior exposure, a mutual contact, or even with a cold call. However, if the buyer hires an intermediary to conduct an exhaustive search, prepare a list of firms that fit the profile of the target acquisition, and make a preliminary contact with those firms on the buyer's behalf, then the buyer's identity does not have to be disclosed until the seller is ready to sign a confidentiality agreement. We'll take a closer look at confidentiality agreements at the end of this chapter, but for now, let's focus on what exactly a buyer needs to do to conduct a comprehensive search.

Buyer's Step #1: Prepare a List of Potential Sellers

The first step is to build a target list of potential sellers. The objective is to systematically identify as many firms as possible that meet the acquisition criteria, although the number of firms targeted will vary depending on the criteria parameters. The industry knowledge and database access of a management consulting firm is often critical in providing the buyer with as many choices as possible.

Buyer's Step #2: Assemble a List of Presidents and CEOs

After you are satisfied that you have found all of the firms that fit your criteria, you should confirm by phone the exact name, title, and mailing address of the president or CEO of each company. All of the information should then be compiled in a database— an intermediary should include this information in a report to the buyer that describes the selection process and lists all of the companies that will be targeted. The buyer should carefully review this list and delete any firms that are not of interest.

Buyer's Step #3: Contact the Approved Target Firms

Step #3 involves sending a confidential letter to each targeted firm's president or CEO. The letter should not divulge the identity of the buyer, but simply seek to determine if the targeted firm is interested in pursuing a discussion with the buyer. The letter should request that if the recipient is interested in selling, he or she should contact the sender (either the buyer or the intermediary) by phone. Each president or CEO who does not respond to the letter should be contacted to determine if an interest exists— sometimes a good opportunity will sit on the desk of an interested but very busy seller, just waiting for someone to "get to it."

Buyer's Step #4: Profile Interested Parties

The buyer or the intermediary should then talk with each party who has expressed an interest in the opportunity to sell. A detailed profile should be prepared for each party that responds and meets the acquisition criteria, and the interviewer should request information on the prospective seller, including general marketing brochures, a client description, financial statements and a Form

Buyer's Steps in Locating a Seller

Figure 5-6

Here is a summary of the steps that we recommend buyers use to locate a firm that is interested in selling.

Step #1: Prepare a List of Potential Sellers

Step #2: Assemble a List of Presidents & CEOs

Step #3: Contact the Approved Target Firms

Step #4: Profile Interested Parties

Step #5: Arrange Preliminary Talks

254, if available. Figure 5-7 lists the information buyers should gather when profiling prospective sellers, and a form to assist with the collection of that information can be found in Appendix A.

Using the information attained in the profiles, the acquisition targets should be ranked according to how well they fit the transaction partner criteria, and how motivated they are to sell. Firms can be easily classified in four categories: strong fit/high interest, weak fit/high interest, strong fit/low interest, and weak fit/low interest. This is the order in which these firms should be pursued.

Buyer's Step #5: Arrange Preliminary Talks

The buyer (or the intermediary, on behalf of the buyer) should next arrange preliminary telephone conversations or meetings with the firms that the buyer decides it would like to pursue, beginning with the strong fit/high interest firms, and then moving to the weak fit/high interest and strong fit/low interest firms. The category of lowest priority is, of course, weak fit/low interest firms.

Information Buyers Should Gather When Profiling Prospective Sellers

Figure 5-7

Once you have decided which firms you want to pursue, it is important to ask questions that will help you decide if they are good match for your firm. Use this list to guide you through profiling a prospective seller.

- Complete firm name
- Addresses and phone numbers of all offices, including headquarters and branch offices
- Name and title of contact person
- Staff size, composition, and qualifications
- How long the firm has been in business
- Owners and corporate structure
- Information on services
- Information on clients
- Project experience
- Computer hardware, software, and networking information
- What assets the firm has and what they're worth
- Professional liability information
- General revenue and profit information for the last three years
- Information on the firm's debt
- Backlog
- Motivation for the owner(s) to sell
- Other

Interest vs. Fit Figure 5-8

In conducting a search for a prospective buyer or seller, you should have two principal questions in mind about each target firm: *How closely do the target firm's size, services, and clients meet the buyer's/seller's criteria?* and *How interested is the target firm's ownership in discussing a potential sale or merger?* To compare each firm's response in terms of these two questions, it's helpful to categorize the firms into the following four groups: Strong fit/High interest, Weak fit/High interest, Strong fit/Low interest, and Weak fit/Low interest.

FIT \ INTEREST	HIGH	LOW
STRONG	First Priority	Third Priority
WEAK	Second Priority	Fourth Priority

Strong fit/High interest: These are firms that meet (or come very close to meeting) your criteria for size, services, and clients, and who are open to talking about a sale or merger. These are your best prospects.

Weak fit/High interest: These are firms that do not completely meet the basic criteria, or have certain issues that are not desirable, but have some features that may interest you. They are open to talking about a sale or merger. These are secondary possibilities.

Strong fit/Low interest: These are firms that meet your criteria for size, services, and clients, but are not as highly motivated as the firms included in the high interest groups. Consider these firms borderline prospects.

Weak fit/Low interest: These are firms that do not meet the basic criteria (although they may have some features that interest you), or are not open to talking seriously about a sale or merger. These firms should be your lowest priority.

Before we discuss these preliminary talks, let's take a look at the search we recommend for sellers. It is similar to the process for buyers, except that it involves developing a prospectus that will be used to market the seller to potential buyers.

For Sellers: Identifying Potential Buyers

The goal in the seller's process is similar to the goal in the buyer's process— to bring as many interested buyers as possible to the seller's attention. The process begins with developing a list of potential buyers.

Sellers are usually much more concerned than buyers about keeping their identity a secret. Unlike buyers, sellers conducting a search on their own are not in good a position to contact potential buyers directly— they risk scaring away clients and employees. We recommend strongly that sellers protect their confidentiality by using an intermediary to contact potential buyers on the seller's behalf. This allows the seller to review the list of interested buyers before choosing to reveal its desire to sell— the seller's identity is not disclosed until the buyer is ready to sign a confidentiality agreement. As we mentioned in the buyer's section, we'll thoroughly review confidentiality agreements later on in this chapter. Let's look now at what sellers need to do to conduct a comprehensive search.

Seller's Step #1: Prepare a List of Potential Buyers

The first step for the seller (or the seller's intermediary) is to build a target list of potential buyers— the number will vary depending on the criteria the seller has determined. The list should include leading firms in the seller's service area; firms who may be interested in the seller's services, geographic location, and/or specialty markets; firms who meet your criteria and have expressed interest in acquiring a firm; and firms who have grown through a merger or acquisition in the past. The experience and industry knowledge of a consultant is often critical when buyers are identifying potential buyers.

Seller's Step #2: Assemble a List of Presidents and CEOs

Next, the exact name, title, and mailing address of the president or CEO of each company should be confirmed by phone. Once this has been completed, all of the information should be compiled in a database, and a report should be produced which describes the research that was conducted and lists all of the target companies identified. This list should be reviewed and approved by the seller. Any firms that the seller does not want to contact (either on its own or through an intermediary) because of known differences in corporate culture, past working relationships, or personality conflicts should be removed from the list.

Seller's Step #3: Contact the Approved Target Firms

The seller or the intermediary will then develop an introductory letter that describes the seller in general terms without divulging the seller's identity. If the seller is to remain anonymous, then the letter should request that all inquiries be directed to the intermediary who will field calls and answer questions on behalf of the seller.

Seller's Step #4: Profile Interested Parties

The next step is to develop a profile for each target company who expresses a sincere interest in the opportunity, including the firm name and contact person, office location and number of employees, a description of their services and client types, their corporate structure and annual revenues. Each president or CEO who does not respond to the letter should be contacted— one or two follow-up calls after the letter are helpful to determine if an interest exists, as many presidents/CEOs are very busy and can be difficult to contact.

Once all of the profiles have been completed, they should be categorized according to their level of interest and their level of compatibility with the seller's original criteria. The seller (and the intermediary) should then review the entire list of interested parties and eliminate any that the seller does not want to enter into discussions with. Figure 5-9 lists the information sellers should gather when profiling prospective buyers, and a form to assist with the collection of that information can be found in Appendix B.

Seller's Step #5: Develop a Prospectus

The purpose of the prospectus is to accurately profile the selling firm for interested buyers. All pertinent information about the company should be presented, highlighting the strengths of the firm and articulating the opportunities the sale provides for a buyer. A wide variety of data is presented in the prospectus, including an overview and history of the firm, professional services, staff profiles, a summary of ownership and reasons for selling, preliminary financial information (including revenues, profits, and backlog), a geographic breakdown of services, the desired structure of the deal, a description of the existing client base, and any marketing materials which serve to give potential clients an orientation to the firms services, standards, and expertise. The document should be developed by the consultant and then reviewed by the seller. A sample prospectus outline can be found in Figure 5-10.

Seller's Step #6: Send a Confidentiality Agreement and Prospectus

Before sending the prospectus to potential buyers, it is wise for sellers to require interested parties to sign a confidentiality agreement. (This agreement is discussed at length later in the chapter.) A cover letter sent with the agreement will

Information Sellers Should Gather When Profiling Prospective Buyers Figure 5-9

Once you have decided which firms you want to talk with, it is important to ask questions that will help you decide if they are good match for your firm. Use this list to guide you through profiling a prospective buyer.

- Complete firm name
- Addresses and phone numbers of all offices, including headquarters and branch offices
- Name and title of contact person
- Staff size
- Annual revenues
- Description of services
- Description of client types
- Owners and corporate structure
- Ideal acquisition opportunity for their firm
- Buyer's reason for exploring this opportunity
- Things buyer sees as negatives in a transaction
- Previous acquisitions
- Other

Sample Prospectus Outline

Figure 5-10

A prospectus provides information about the selling firm to interested buyers. The following outline will help you to assemble the information that prospective buyers will want to know about your firm.

Preamble - Identification

The names of all entities (corporations, limited liability companies, partnerships, etc.) are listed along with the name of the intermediary.

Overview

The overview is a description of the entities, including areas of expertise, general overview of types of clients, number of employees, revenues, geographic location of offices and practices (both foreign and domestic), and general reputation of the entities.

Corporate History

The corporate history section gives a summary of the history of the firm, including year of founding, founders, expansion, growth and reasons, backlog, and future prospects.

Reasons to Sell or Merge

The underlying motivations for selling should be addressed, which may include articulating the firm's need for ownership transition, expansion, capital expenditures, new geographic markets, new areas of expertise, etc.

Corporate Status and Ownership

This section includes a description of each entity, its legal status, stockholders, and directors. If an ESOP is involved, it should be addressed here, as well as all other fiduciary stockholders.

Office Locations

Include the address of each office, along with a brief description of the number of employees, activities of the office, and the person in charge of the location.

Services

A detailed description of the types of services offered should be given. Be sure to note significant delivery methods such as design-build.

Clients

A general description of the types of clients the firm serves, along with a detailed listing of actual clients, billings, and percent of total revenue. Significant recent clients and projects should be noted, along with any allied design professionals.

Professional Staff

The principals of the firm should be described in some detail. An organization chart and listing of personnel should also be included.

Financial Summary

It is important that the prospectus also contain financial information in the form of financial statements (income and balance sheet), along with backlog. Any available analysis describing the breakdown in revenues is useful. Assets and leases should be described.

Awards and Professional Recognition

Any awards that the firm has received should be noted with a brief description.

Seller's Steps in Locating a Buyer

Figure 5-11

Here is a summary of the steps that we recommend sellers use to locate a buyer for their firm.

Step #1: Prepare a List of Potential Buyers

Step #2: Assemble a List of Presidents & CEOs

Step #3: Contact the Approved Target Firms

Step #4: Profile Interested Parties

Step #5: Develop a Prospectus

Step #6: Send Confidentiality Agreement and Prospectus

Step #7: Arrange Preliminary Talks

finally reveal the name of the selling firm to potential buyers, and the seller or intermediary should only send a copy of the prospectus to interested buyers who execute the confidentiality agreement. Because the name of the seller is not disclosed up to this point, the seller will have had complete control over its exposure during the search process, especially if contact with interested buyers has been handled by an intermediary.

Seller's Step #7: Arrange Preliminary Talks

Once potential buyers have had a chance to review the prospectus, the seller or intermediary should arrange preliminary telephone conversations or personal meetings between the seller and each of the parties who are still interested. During this process, it behooves the seller to retain the intermediary to field questions and concerns from prospective buyers and then to relay important information back to the seller.

Now that we have reviewed the search process from the perspective of both the buyer and seller, we bring the focus back to the two parties together as they meet each other for the first time.

The First Meeting

The players at the kickoff meeting are one or two of the most senior principals from both firms— and the intermediary if one is involved. Having the meeting over lunch or dinner helps to set a get-to-know-you tone for the initial discussion where the objective is for the principals to meet each other and determine whether or not their personal styles are compatible. A general discussion of why each party is interested in the deal is appropriate, as perhaps a principal in the selling firm is retiring, or the buying firm is looking for geographical expansion in the seller's area.

If all goes smoothly at the initial meeting, a second meeting will likely follow. Be sure to clearly communicate the impression you want to leave with your prospective partner at these meetings, and to try to get a handle on the more nebulous

> ### *War Story: Fancy Car*
> Figure 5-12
>
> AN ATTORNEY was once asked to attend the second meeting of a client with a prospective transaction partner. The client, prior to the arrival of the other party, expressed a concern that the seller's owner was a bit flamboyant and perhaps would not fit as a team player in the buyer's culture. As the client spoke, the seller pulled into the parking lot in full view of all the attorney and client in a $60,000 sports car. The other cars in the lot were late model, medium-priced automobiles owned by the buyer's senior managers. At that moment, the cultural misfit was identified and the deal went no further. The meeting had achieved its purpose by determining that future discussions were unwarranted.

people-aspects of the firm you talking with. Finally, from the outset, clearly define your goals and articulate the characteristics of a successful purchase or sale. This will allow both parties to understand exactly what the other expects, should the negotiations lead to an actual transaction.

Regardless of who initiates the discussion, these initial meetings are often a cause of great apprehension for both buyers and sellers. How you approach them can make all the difference in the world, and the old cliché "You only get one chance to make a good first impression" holds true. Above all, be yourself and be truthful. The goal at this stage in the relationship is simply to try to understand each other's needs, wants, plans, and expectations.

Feedback Meetings With Intermediary

Another benefit of involving an intermediary is that you can sit down after the meeting to talk about the positives, negatives, and questions that came out of the initial contacts. Intermediaries can offer an objective opinion about the interaction of the principals and the compatibility of the firms.

At this point, the intermediary can help you evaluate whether to continue or terminate discussions. Are both parties enthused about getting into the more substantial terms of the deal, or was there a cultural rift that made both parties uneasy? If the buyer or seller (or both) are inclined to cut off the discussions, then the parties should move on and nothing is lost. A word of caution however. Some firms (and their principals) become so intrigued with the idea of generally discussing a deal that no progress is made toward the substantive terms of a transaction. Don't waste the effort of having several more general discussions. One or two initial meetings should establish whether the discussions should proceed further with substantive and more focused negotiations. If irreconcilable personal or differences emerge, however, end the discussions and move on. You shouldn't waste the effort or the time you could spend pursuing other opportunities.

The Confidentiality Agreement

Now let's take a closer look at the confidentiality agreement, which is sometimes called a confidential memorandum or a non-disclosure and confidentiality agreement. A confidentiality agreement is a quid pro quo ("you scratch my back, I'll scratch yours") arrangement, where the right of access to information is given by one firm in exchange for a right to access the second firm's information. The agreement basically says that all information obtained during the preliminary due diligence review will be kept confidential and will not be used in a competitive manner.

In order for the discussion to take on a more substantive form, both parties must begin to exchange more specific and detailed information about their respective firms. The greatest concern for both buyers and sellers at this point is that all information that is exchanged be kept confidential, and so a reciprocal confidentiality agreement that binds both parties becomes appropriate. The objective of the confidentiality agreement is to allow a free and productive exchange of information between the parties.

In reality, however, the confidentiality agreement is only worth the word of the parties who sign it— in other words, if you're dealing with another trustworthy party that's great, but if you're dealing with an unscrupulous character, the agreement may not be air tight. In any case, you should be prepared for the possibility that confidential information will get out, and it's up to you to find a way to confront, contain, or put a positive spin on it.

Confidentiality Agreement Provisions

At a minimum, the confidentiality agreement should include the following:

- a definition of what information is considered to be confidential;
- a provision that the confidential information will be kept confidential, and may only be used for the purpose of evaluating the proposed transaction;
- a provision that the confidential information may only be disclosed to certain eligible persons who also agree to keep such information confidential (typically, the recipient's accountants, financing sources, lawyers, investment bankers and employees);
- a provision that if the parties decide not to proceed with the negotiations they will return all copies of the confidential information to the other party;
- allowances for certain exceptions to confidentiality obligations (i.e., where

Leaky Confidentiality Agreements Figure 5-13

Warning: Most M&A discussions take place under the apparent security of a confidentiality agreement. Although they sound formal, not everyone takes confidentiality agreements seriously. It is unrealistic to expect that nothing will leak out, and the agreements are often not worth the paper they're written on.

For example, someone called up a potential seller and said they were interested in buying the firm. They weren't really, but they got information about the sellers employees and then recruited them. The moral of the story is don't get into detailed discussions with people you haven't screened or don't trust. Be realistic that information will get out, and expect that word might get around. And when it does, do what you can to minimize bad press and put a positive spin on any leaked information.

the confidential information becomes publicly available through no fault of the recipient or where the recipient becomes legally obligated to disclose the confidential information, subject to any right of the disclosing party to intervene to challenge or mitigate such disclosure requirement); and

- a provision that in the event of a breach or threatened breach by the recipient of the confidential information, the disclosing party will be entitled to seek injunctive relief.

It is in the best interest of both parties to keep the scope of the confidentiality and non-competition provisions as narrow as possible. Items that are meant to be kept confidential should be expressly identified as such. In addition, one or both parties may want to include a further provision to address situations in which certain items will no longer be subject to the agreement. This may include matters ceasing to be confidential as the result of public disclosure (but not resulting from the other party's disclosure) or according to litigation between the buyer and seller.

It is not unusual for special disclosure issues to arise in some deals. For example, sellers are often unwilling to disclose some kinds or information like client lists, and they may not permit a buyer to contact existing clients or vendors until a definitive purchase and sale agreement is signed (or at least until there is an agreement on price and other material terms in a letter of intent). This is most common in situations where the buyer and seller are competitors prior to the negotiations. In addition, the seller will not want its employees, suppliers or clients to know that it is negotiating a sale, particularly in cases where the business could be damaged if the deal fell through.

If the buyer and the seller address these issues up front and agree upon procedures for the due diligence investigation, the exchange of information will not be as difficult. These procedures may include (i) postponing the most sensitive due diligence until the definitive acquisition agreements or a letter of intent are

Confidentiality Agreement Provision Checklist Figure 5-14

The following provisions should be included in a confidentiality agreement.

- Definition of what information is considered confidential
- Clause that confidential information will be kept confidential and used only to evaluate the transaction
- Clause stating that only certain eligible persons who also agree to keep the information confidential will have access to it
- Provision that all copies of the information will be returned if the transaction is terminated
- Exceptions to confidentiality obligations
- Clause stating that the disclosing party is entitled to injunctive relief in the event of a breach or threatened breach by the recipient

Sample Confidentiality Agreement Figure 5-15

A confidentiality agreement is a standard agreement where the right to access to information is given by one firm in exchange for a right to access the second firm's information. The agreement basically says that all information will be kept confidential and will not be used in a competitive manner.

CONFIDENTIALITY AGREEMENT

THIS AGREEMENT is made as of the _____ day of ____________, ______, between ABC, Inc. ("ABC") of ____________________ and XYZ, Inc. ("XYZ") of _______________________.

WHEREAS the parties wish to discuss a possible business combination between them (herein referred to as the "Discussions"); and

WHEREAS each of the parties has developed certain "Confidential Information" (as defined below) which relates to its business and which it may be necessary or desirable to disclose in the Discussions; and

WHEREAS the parties wish to protect and use and/or disclosure of the Confidential Information during the Discussions and thereafter;

NOW, THEREFORE, in consideration of the premises and the mutual covenants contained herein, it is agreed, as follows:

1. Except as is reasonably necessary for the purposes of the Discussions, neither party shall use, either directly or indirectly, any Confidential Information of the other.

2. Neither party shall disclose to other any Confidential Information, either directly or indirectly, except as is reasonably necessary for the purposes of the Discussions.

3. The foregoing obligation shall pertain to the use or disclosure by the parties or by any of their respective affiliates, subsidiaries, officers, directors, stockholders, employees, agents, independent contractors and/or any others receiving Confidential Information from, by or through them.

4. "Confidential Information" means any information disclosed to a party after the date hereof during or as a result of the Discussions, which is not readily available to the general public and which is clearly marked or otherwise identified as confidential at the time of disclosure and relates to the business of the party or to the party's customers or suppliers, whether such information is of a technical or a business nature, and includes, without limitation, purchase orders, customer contracts, assets and liabilities, trade secrets, research projects, proposals, computer programs, financial information, billing rates, tax returns, business or marketing methods or plans, and inventions and improvements thereto. "Confidential Information" does not include information known to a party prior to the date hereof or prior to obtaining it from the disclosing party, information in the public domain at the time of disclosure, or information obtained from a third party who to such party's knowledge has no obligation of secrecy with respect thereto.

5. In the event of the termination of the Discussions for any reason, the parties agree to return all copies of the Confidential Information to each other.

(Continued on next page.)

Figure 5-15 cont.

6. The confidentiality obligations set forth herein are in addition to and not in derogation of (a) any rights otherwise secured to the parties by law or contract; and (b) any rights or trust, confidence or ethical duty otherwise imposed by law. Each party agrees that the covenants contained herein are fair and reasonably required for the protection of the other's business. It is also understood and agreed that any violation of these covenants may cause irreparable harm and damage to the other party, which would not adequately be compensated by money damages and therefore the party shall be entitled to injunctive relief, in addition to any other remedies provided by law or in equity, for such violation.

IN WITNESS WHEREOF, the parties have executed this agreement as of the date first above written.

ABC, Inc.

By: ______________________________

XYZ, Inc.

By: ______________________________

signed (in these situations, each party's obligation to close is usually subject to satisfactory completion of due diligence), or (ii) performing most of the due diligence off-site and having limited contact with the other firm's employees so as to minimize the number of people who become aware of the negotiations. In the end, the buyer's need to perform a satisfactory due diligence investigation must be balanced against the seller's disclosure concerns, and some jockeying may be required to find a happy medium.

A sample confidentiality agreement can be found in Figure 5-15. The firms' lawyers usually draft and negotiate this agreement. A special word of caution, however, if the parties to the confidentiality agreement compete with each other in geographical areas: it is important that the confidentiality agreement include a provision that expressly acknowledges such competition and that any disclosure of client lists does not preclude either party from seeking work from clients of the other party. In other words, non-competition provisions are not appropriate at this stage in the discussions. Another concern between parties that often arises has to do with recruiting. The parties may wish to include a provision that neither will hire an employee of the other within a certain time period after signing the confidentiality agreement. Often, however, the agreement is a straightforward, simple document that provides for a reciprocal exchange of information.

Conclusion

Choosing how to conduct a search process for interested buyers or sellers is a critical decision in the deal process. There are a number of ways to identify transaction partners, although the most successful search processes are comprehensive searches conducted by intermediaries that have experience in the industry.

As the parties sign confidentiality agreements and begin exchanging preliminary information, the search phase leads to more substantive discussions with one (or a few) of the targeted firms. Before moving on to the letter of intent in Chapter 7, this is a good time to stop and consider the corporate and tax aspects in structuring a merger or acquisition, which is the focus of Chapter 6.

6 Corporate & Tax Considerations

- Introduction
- Stock or Asset Transfer?
- Tax Aspects of Ownership Transfer
- Taxable Transactions
  - Taxable Sale of Stock
  - Taxable Sale of Assets
- Tax-Free or Tax-Deferred Transactions
  - Statutory Merger (“A” Reorganization)
  - Stock-for-Stock (“B” Reorganization)
  - Assets-for-Stock (“C” Reorganization)
- Requirements for All Tax-Free Transactions
  - Business Purpose and Plan of Reorganization
  - Continuity of Business Enterprise
  - Continuity of Interest
- Step Transaction
- Securities Law Aspects of an Exchange of Stock
- Consulting and Employment Agreements
- Stock Ownership in Buyer
- Conclusion

Chapter 6

Corporate and Tax Considerations

☑ *Before you can decide how the deal will be structured, you first have to think about whether the transaction will be a stock and/or asset transfer, whether the transfer will be taxable or nontaxable to the seller, and whether future service or non-competition agreements with the seller's principals will be part of the compensation.*

Introduction

Once you've identified some potential transaction partners, you're all set to move on to the preliminary discussions and negotiating the letter of intent. But before we move ahead, this is a good point to take a break and clarify a few details regarding the corporate and tax aspects of a merger or acquisition. Be warned—this is a long and somewhat tedious chapter, written to give you some perspective on the part of the deal that is usually handled by accountants and attorneys. For readers who become weary halfway through, take heart— understanding the different ways of structuring a deal could save you money in the long run. So stand up, jog in place, get a Coke, and then hunker down as we plunge into the world of corporate and tax issues.

When the buyer and seller begin to review confidential information as part of preliminary due diligence, the basic structure of the transaction becomes an important consideration. Planning what the final deal will look like, and how the goals of the buyer and seller will be achieved, depends on the advice of the advising attorneys, financial advisors, and accountants, since the issues are both complex and technical in nature.

So how do you go about beginning to sketch out the form of the transaction? The deal structure can initially be outlined based on the form of the transfer of ownership (a transfer of the seller's assets or equity of the firm's stockholders). In addition, both parties must agree on the consideration to be paid by the buyer (cash, notes, and/or stock), whether the transaction will be taxable or nontaxable to the seller and/or its stockholders, whether any of the seller's employees will receive employment agreements, and whether any of the seller's senior employees will receive consulting agreements as a transition to retirement, and lastly, whether any employees of the seller are being offered ownership in the buyer.

This section is meant to provide readers with an overview of the corporate and tax issues that arise as the structure of the final deal begins to unfold. It is by no means meant to give a buyer or seller all the information necessary to negotiate the structure of a particular deal without the proper legal and financial advice.

Stock or Asset Transfer?

There are two ways of transferring ownership of an A/E/P or environmental consulting firm: the seller's stockholders can transfer stock to the buyer, or the seller can simply transfer assets.

Pros and Cons of Stock Deals for Buyers and Sellers

Figure 6-1

Knowing the pros and cons of a stock deal can help you decide if this kind of transaction is right for your firm. Buyers and sellers can use this chart to navigate the benefits and downfalls of stock deals.

BUYER		SELLER	
Pros	**Cons**	**Pros**	**Cons**
The transaction is simple: the buyer gains all of the seller's assets by purchasing the seller's stock for cash or other consideration.	The buyer gains all of the seller's liabilities by purchasing the stock.	The transaction is simple: the buyer gains all of the seller's assets by purchasing the seller's stock for cash or other consideration.	The transaction may require SEC registration.
Can be executed without the agreement of the management of the seller.	Tax treatment remains unchanged (and the buyer inherits the seller's tax attributes).	Management and minority stockholders can not stop individual stockholders from selling their stock to the buyer (absent transfer restrictions).	Consideration paid by the buyer may include the buyer's stock in lieu of or in addition to cash or cash equivalents.
All of the seller's equity interest is assigned to the buyer.		In selling the stock, the seller transfers all liabilities to the buyer.	
No consents to transfer leases or client contracts are required.		No consents to transfer leases or client contracts are required.	
The buyer may pay the seller in stock rather than or in addition to cash or cash equivalents.		One level of tax at stockholder level— typically capital gain.	

Stock Transfer

A stock transfer involves assigning to the buyer all (or a supermajority) of the equity interest (voting stock, non-voting stock, and preferred stock) of the seller by its stockholders. By purchasing the stock, the buyer gains all of the seller's assets (including cash and accounts receivable), subject to all of the seller's liabilities, including those that are known and unknown, direct or contingent. Most buyers are very cautious about the assumption of such liabilities, and rightly so.

Since the buyer wants to own all of the equity, a stock transaction usually requires the transfer of 100% of the stock. On the down side, such a requirement gives any minority stockholder of the seller leverage to hold-up or kill the deal. Stock deals do, however, have the distinct advantage of not requiring any consents to transfer contracts and leases (except in the limited cases where there is a specific change of control provision in the documents), since there is no change in the organization of the seller. With a stock transaction, therefore, a very time-consuming process is eliminated, and there is no risk that a client will not consent to the assignment of the contract.

Asset Transfer

An asset transfer allows the parties to negotiate which assets will be transferred, and only the assets specified are assigned by the seller to the buyer. If you are the seller, then it is likely that you will want to retain cash and accounts receivable. And if you're the buyer, you will probably assume only those liabilities that are specified, leaving contingent and unknown liabilities with the seller. Under this arrangement, the buyer usually winds up with goodwill (like the company name and telephone number), specified fixed assets, and all contracts. Of course, since assets are being transferred, in most cases consents to transfer client contracts and leases will be required by each client or lessor.

Tax Aspects of Ownership Transfer

A corporate transaction may be structured as (i) a taxable acquisition, (ii) a nontaxable transaction, or (iii) a partially taxable acquisition. Under each of these general alternatives, the buyer and the seller (or its stockholders) may agree to either a sale of seller's assets or a sale of the stock by its stockholders. In a taxable acquisition, the stockholders may either sell stock to the buyer or cause the seller to sell assets to the buyer. In a nontaxable or partially taxable acquisition where all or part of the seller's gain is deferred, the stockholders may either exchange their stock or cause the seller to exchange its assets for stock of the buyer.

Taxable Transactions

There are two basic types of taxable transactions: a taxable sale of stock, and a taxable sale of assets.

Taxable Sale of Stock

The stockholders who receive cash and/or notes from the buyer in a taxable acquisition of their stock will generally recognize gain or loss by measuring the difference between the fair market value of what they receive, and the basis in their shares, which normally is what they paid for it (unless the seller ran the company as an S corporation, where the basis rules are much more complicated). The stockholders should generally qualify for capital gain or loss treatment on the sale of their stock.

Pros and Cons of Asset Deals for Buyers and Sellers

Figure 6-2

Knowing the pros and cons of an asset deal can help you decide if this kind of transaction is right for your firm. Buyers and sellers can use this chart to navigate the benefits and downfalls of asset deals.

BUYER		SELLER	
Pros	**Cons**	**Pros**	**Cons**
Buyer can choose which assets will be transferred and which liabilities will be assumed.	Transaction is complex because every asset must be transferred separately.	Seller can choose to retain cash accounts and A/R.	Transaction is complex because every asset must be transferred separately.
Tax basis in acquired assets increase, which should enhance future tax deductions.	Consents to transfer leases and client contracts are required.	A more liquid transaction than a stock deal–consideration is usually paid in cash or cash equivalents.	Consents to transfer client contracts and leases are required.
	Transaction is subject to state and local transfer taxes.		Transaction is subject to state and local transfer taxes.
	Greater potential for disruption of clients and contracts.		Potential double level of tax (corporate and stockholder level).

Since there is currently a tax rate differential limiting the maximum capital gain to 28% (in contrast with the marginal federal rate of 39.6% for earned income), stockholders will most likely want to receive most of their purchase price in return for their stock— not for consulting and non-compete agreements and other payments that are generally deductible or amortizable by the buyer but taxed as ordinary income to the stockholders. Most significantly, a stock sale will result in only one level of tax to the stockholders, since there is no corporate-level tax. And if the buyer's consideration includes notes in addition to cash, a number of complex issues are raised for stockholders concerning a possible deferral of taxable gain under the installment method of recognition of income.

Taxable Sale of Assets

In a taxable purchase of assets, the buyer purchases all or substantially all of the seller's assets for cash and/or notes and the seller liquidates. Such a transaction is accomplished either by a traditional asset sale, or in a state law two-party merger of the seller into the buyer, where the consideration is cash and/or notes, but not stock in the buyer. In addition to the transfer of any liabilities, the buyer would take a basis in the seller's assets equal to the purchase price of those assets. The ability to assume only certain specified liabilities and to obtain a new cost basis in the assets purchased could be major advantages for the buyer of an asset sale over a stock sale (in the case of a traditional asset sale, but not a merger).

The seller will be taxed on the full gain or loss in its assets (including goodwill), regardless of whether it immediately liquidates. The seller can generally postpone being taxed on the gain on the sale of certain capital gain assets, but only to the extent that the seller receives notes from the buyer. If the seller does liquidate, the stockholders will be fully taxed on any gain or loss realized on the return of their shares (the excess of the cash and fair value of property received by the stockholders over their basis is their capital gain). If the seller were to distribute notes of the buyer in an immediate liquidation, stockholders generally may report the portion of their liquidation gain attributable to the notes on the installment method.

The major disadvantage of a taxable sale of assets from the seller's stockholders' perspective is that (unless the seller is an S corporation), an asset sale will result in two levels of taxation. The seller's stockholders will only receive about 30% of the cash, or cash and notes, proceeds net after taxes (with 70% going for taxes), since in a taxable asset transaction their gains are subject to both corporate and personal taxes.

Tax-Free or Tax-Deferred Transactions

The tax rules that govern whether a specific transaction will be tax-free or tax-deferred are quite complex and must be adhered to precisely, so again, we stress that the general nature of this discussion is not meant to replace consulting tax counsel on each individual transaction.

There are several basic structures that avoid current taxation. Although these scenarios are usually referred to as "tax-free" reorganizations, they are more accurately described as "tax-deferred." Since the buyer and the seller pay no income tax on the tax-deferred portion of the consideration at the time of the transaction, their basis in stock or assets does not change. The inherent gain in the transaction is simply postponed and will be taxable only if the stock or assets are later sold in a taxable transaction during their lifetime.

Taxable Transactions

Figure 6-3

This chart outlines the conditions that pertain to a taxable sale of stock and a taxable sale of assets.

Taxable Sale of Stock	■ seller's stockholders recognize gain or loss equal to fair market value of what's received—stockholder's basis in shares ■ stockholders qualify for capital gain or loss taxes on the sale of stock (max. federal capital gain tax rate is 28%) ■ stockholders are only taxed on a personal level—there is no corporate level tax
Taxable Sale of Assets	**If the seller chooses to liquidate:** ■ buyer purchases all of the seller's assets for cash and/or cash equivalents, and the seller liquidates ■ buyer has the advantages of assuming only selected liabilities and getting a new cost-basis in the assets purchased ■ seller is taxed currently on ordinary income assets ■ seller's stockholders are taxed on the gain or loss realized on the return of their shares ■ seller's stockholders can defer portion of gain from buyer's notes distributed in liquidation **If the seller chooses not to liquidate:** ■ taxes on the seller's portion of gain from notes may be postponed

Statutory Merger ("A" Reorganization)

The merger of two corporations, known as an "A" reorganization under the Internal Revenue Code, is the most flexible form of tax-free reorganization. To the extent they receive stock of the buyer, no taxable gain is recognized by the stockholders of the seller. Except for the buyer's notes received by the seller's stockholders, all other consideration is taxed upon receipt.

Stock-for-Stock ("B" Reorganization)

In the stock-for-stock form of transaction (the easiest but most inflexible transaction), the seller's stockholders are required to exchange their stock solely for the voting stock of the buyer, and the buyer is "in control" of the seller immediately after the transaction. This type of reorganization is known as a "B" reorganization under the Internal Revenue Code. Because the stockholders can receive only voting stock, they recognize no gain or loss at the time of the transaction.

Assets-for-Stock ("C" Reorganization)

The third type of tax-free reorganization is known as a "C" reorganization. In this case, substantially all of the seller's assets generally are exchanged for solely voting stock of the buyer, which is then distributed to the seller's stockholders in the liquidation of the seller. No taxable gain or loss is recognized by the stockholders of the seller when they receive stock of the buyer. However, if cash or property other than the buyer's stock is distributed to the seller's stockholders, then taxable income may result on those payments unless a minimal amount of the seller's liabilities are assumed by the buyer.

Requirements for All Tax-Free Transactions

Besides the statutory rules that apply to particular types of tax-free transactions, there are a number of additional legal requirements which every tax-free corporate acquisition (known as a reorganization) must satisfy.

Business Purpose and Plan of Reorganization

A reorganization will not be tax-free unless you meet two requirements: there must be a legitimate business purpose for the reorganization, and a written plan of reorganization— both of which are generally easy requirements to meet. A two-page document prepared by the buyer's attorney should outline the non-tax business purpose of the reorganization, and a copy should be retained by both the buyer and the seller in case the IRS ever challenges the reorganization.

Continuity of Business Enterprise

A continuity of the business enterprise exists when the acquiring corporation continues the historic business or uses a significant portion of the selling corporation's historic business assets.

Continuity of Interest

To meet the continuity of interest test, the selling stockholders must acquire a sufficient equity interest in the buyer. According to IRS, to be "sufficient," the equity interest (stock) in the buyer received by the seller's stockholders must equal (in value) at least 50% of the total value in the seller before the transaction.

Tax-Free or Tax-Deferred Transactions

Figure 6-4

This chart outlines the conditions that pertain to tax-free or tax-deferred transactions.

Statutory Merger ("A" Reorganization)	■ flexible form of tax-free reorganization ■ no taxable gain is recognized by the stockholders of the seller to the extent that they receive stock of the buyer ■ gain may be deferred by the stockholders of the seller to the extent they receive notes of the buyer ■ cash consideration is taxed upon receipt
Stock-for-Stock ("B" Reorganization)	■ easiest form of reorganization ■ seller's stockholders exchange their stock solely for voting stock of the buyer ■ immediately after the transaction, the buyer must "control" the seller ■ no gain or loss is recognized by the seller's stockholders at the time of the transaction
Assets-for-Stock ("C" Reorganization)	■ substantially all of the seller's assets are exchanged for voting stock of the buyer ■ this stock is then distributed to the seller's stockholders ■ seller must liquidate ■ sellers do not recognize any gain or loss unless they receive cash or other assets, which are taxable

Step Transaction

A step transaction is one in which a series of transactions that take place in close succession are viewed by the IRS as one transaction. To determine if your transactions may fall into this category, conditions before and after the changes in ownership should be examined, and if the transactions are related, they will be treated as one for tax purposes. The step transaction can have negative consequences when unwanted assets are disposed of before certain types of corporate reorganizations, or where stockholders who receive the buyer's stock immediately dispose of it.

Securities Law Aspects of an Exchange of Stock

This section outlines the securities law issues that are involved in a business acquisition where the seller receives shares of a publicly-held buyer as consideration for the sale of the seller's business.

In a corporation acquisition affected by the issuance of the buyer's securities, the buyer is deemed to have offered its securities for sale. The securities have to be registered under the Securities Act of 1933, and a prospectus must be used in connection with proxy solicitations, provided that there are no available exemptions.

Sale of Unregistered Shares Other Than Through Registration

If unregistered shares are received as part of the combination of businesses, then pursuant to Rule 144 of the Securities Act of 1933, the shares can be resold in the public market in accordance with the following requirements:

(1) the shares must have been held for at least one year following the transaction to combine the businesses (prior to 4/29/97, the shares must have been held for at least **two** years following the transaction to combine the businesses);

(2) the number of shares which can be sold in any three-month period is limited to the greater of

(a)1% of the outstanding shares of that class of securities or

(b) the average weekly reported trading volume of that class of securities over the four weeks prior to any sale;

(3) the shares must be sold to a market maker or in an unsolicited transaction in which the broker acts as an agent for the seller;

(4) the issuer must be current in its SEC reporting obligations; and

(5) if the sale is very large (the threshold is currently 500 shares or $10,000 during any 3 months, but is proposed to be changed to 1,000 shares or $40,000), a Form 144 (which limits how much can be sold) may need to be filed with the SEC in connection with the sale.

If the shares have been held for at least two years following the transaction and the holder is not an affiliate (and has not been so for at least three months), the shares can be freely resold in the public market. (Prior to 4/29/97, shares could be freely resold in the public market if they had been held for at least **three** years following the transaction and the holder was not an affiliate.)

Requirements for Selling Unregistered Shares of Stock in the Public Market

Figure 6-5

If unregistered shares are received as part of the combination of businesses, then pursuant to Rule 144 of the Securities Act of 1933, the shares can be resold in the public market in accordance with the requirements listed below.

1. Shares must have been held for at least one year following the transaction to combine the businesses.

2. The number of share which can be sold in any three month period is limited to the greater of:

- 1% of the outstanding shares of that class of securities, or
- the average weekly reported trading volume of that class of securities over the four weeks prior to the sale.

3. The shares must be sold to a market maker or in an unsolicited transaction in which the broker acts as an agent for the seller.

4. The issuer must be current in its SEC reporting obligations.

5. If the sale is very large a Form 144 may need to be filed with the SEC in connection with the sale.

The second method by which stockholders can sell the shares they receive in the business combination is in a so-called Section 4 (1-1/2) private placement exempt transaction. There is no hard and fast rule regarding how long shares must be held following the business combination and prior to a 4 (1-1/2) sale, but two years is probably a safe holding period. In addition, in order to satisfy this exemption, a purchaser of the shares must acquire them for investment and must possess a level of sophistication which demonstrates that he or she has both sufficient business experience and the economic wherewithal to evaluate the merits and assume the risks of the investment.

Registration Rights

Unless one of the above resale options is selected, a person who acquires shares in a non-public offering must have the shares registered prior to any resale. Since the issuer is the only entity which can register shares, it is important that the seller negotiate some form of contractual commitment from the buyer to register the shares for public sale. This can be either through the seller's stockholders receiving demand registration rights or piggyback registration rights. Demand registration rights essentially permit a stockholder, through the agreement of a certain percentage of the group of stockholders who received their unregistered shares, to require or "demand" at any time that the issuer file a registration statement, and keep it current long enough for the stockholders to sell their shares to the public. Piggyback registration rights require the buyer to notify the stockholders when the buyer is about to file a registration statement. In this case, to the extent that the issuer does not file a registration statement, the stockholders will not be able to sell their shares publicly, except pursuant to one of the exemptions mentioned above. In addition, even if the buyer does file a registration statement, often, to the extent any underwriter involved in the offering relating to such filing believes that the additional shares of the stockholders will impair the offering, the stockholders either may not be able to include their shares in the registration statement at all, or may be limited in the number of shares that may be included. Demand registration rights are, therefore, very important to the seller's stockholders in a business combination involving an exchange of unregistered stock.

Resale of Securities Registered in the Business Combination

If the shares received in a business combination have been registered for sale in the business combination and the stockholder is not an affiliate of either the issuer or the acquired entity, then according to Rule 145 of the Securities Act of 1933, the shares can be freely resold in the public market. To the extent that the stockholder is an affiliate of the issuer, he or she will be subject to Rule 144 in all resales of his or her shares. Stockholders who were affiliates of the acquired entity at the time the business combination was voted on, but who are not affiliates of the issuer, may make resales as follows:

(a) at any time in accordance with all of the above mentioned Rule 144 provisions, except the holding period and Form 144 requirements;

(b) freely after one year following the date of acquisition of the securities, so long as the issuer meets the public information requirements of Rule 144 (Prior to 4/29/97, stockholders who were affiliates of the acquired entity at the time the business combination was voted on, but who were not affiliates of the issuer, could make resales freely after two years following the date of acquisition of the securities.); and

(c) freely after two years following the date of acquisition of the securities, as long as the person has not been an affiliate of the issuer for at least three months. (Prior to 4/29/97, stockholders who were affiliates of the acquired entity at the time the business combination was voted on, but who were not affiliates of the issuer for at least three months, could make resales freely after three years following the date of acquisition of the securities.)

In some cases, there may also be tax or accounting issues associated with a particular transaction which may prevent or delay a resale by a stockholder.

The analysis of the tax and corporate aspects to a transaction is highly technical, subject to the changes in the applicable laws from time to time, and in each case dependent on the specific set of facts. The tax professionals in the law firm representing a party, together with the business lawyer and the firm's accountant, must work together in massaging the corporate and tax parameters of a transaction into a sensible approach that will meet the business goals of the primary deal.

Consulting Agreements

In addition to paying for the purchase of assets or shares, the buyer may enter into a consulting agreement with one or more of the seller's stockholders. If the buyer wishes to keep a senior stockholder for only a short transition period, then this may be an attractive offer for the stockholder. The consulting agreement can cover a period of one or more years, and it may stipulate that compensation will, at least in part, be based on the performance of the seller's clients. Since they are deductible for the buyer, the payments are taxed to the stockholder as ordinary income. This is also an attractive option for the buyer, since consideration for the transaction is paid over time and is tax deductible.

The buyer may also want to structure the agreement so that future restrictions are placed on the consultant to prevent competing with the buyer and/or soliciting the employees of the buyer.

Employment Agreements

Buyers will usually want to make sure that key stockholders and senior managers will stay on after the transaction. As the old adage states, "the assets go home every night." Therefore, employment arrangements with key personnel are to be anticipated. The buyer can also add provisions to this agreement to protect against the solicitation of employees and clients for a period of time after employment is terminated. Thus, the buyer has again managed to pay some of the transaction cost over time, without interest, in tax-deductible dollars, and while obtaining some business protection— all in all, not a bad idea.

Depending on whether the buyer is a private of a public company, these issues will vary greatly.

Stock Ownership in Buyer

Many of the seller's stockholders may want to become stockholders of the buyer, either initially (at the closing of the transaction) or at some later point. To these stockholders, the terms of the "buy in" to own stock in the buyer, the stockholders' agreement which governs the buyout of stockholders of the buyer, and the general terms of being a stockholder and principal of the buyer are critical, and should be thoroughly reviewed.

Conclusion

Structuring a merger or acquisition deal depends on whether the parties decide on a transfer of stock, assets, or both, and whether the transaction will be taxable or non-taxable. With the help of your attorney, accountant, and financial advisor, you will be able to analyze each option, and decide which one is the best for your firm.

Once the corporate and tax aspects of the deal have been decided, and the parties have reached an agreement on the role of employment, consulting, and non-compete agreements in the deal, it is time to move on to drafting the letter of intent, which is the topic of Chapter 7.

7 The Letter of Intent

The Letter of Intent

☑ *Sometimes referred to as a "term sheet" or "memorandum of understanding," the letter of intent is the document that outlines the major points of the transaction. The primary topic of the letter of intent is a determination of the purchase price, although it should address all of the fundamental aspects of the deal.*

Introduction

Congratulations! You've made it through the most difficult chapter in the book, and now it's time to get back to the transaction process. When we left Chapter 5, the parties had just signed a confidentiality agreement, and were beginning to exchange basic information about their firms and their transaction objectives.

There are two basic goals in exchanging preliminary information. First, there is an interest in identifying any deal-breakers or structural information which might cause one party to back out and decide not to pursue the deal. Second, each firm needs to confirm their profile of the transaction partner and what is needed to make the transaction successful. This exchange of basic information begins the process of outlining the deal— the precursor to the formal letter of intent. In this exchange, the parties must also explore and understand several topics which help dictate whether there is a good "fit" between the firms:

- What is the corporate culture of each firm?
- How will the surviving entity be governed?
- Will the name of seller be used?
- How will the firms integrate at the operational level? At the marketing level?
- Will HR, administration and finance be merged to obtain operating synergy?
- Will the seller remain an autonomous operating entity with an independent identity?
- Will offices of the seller be closed?
- How will the employees of each firm view the transaction?
- Will some employees of the seller be terminated? If so, what type of severance package will be offered?

Once these issues have been generally resolved, the parties are ready to move on to drafting the letter of intent.

Checklist for Preliminary Exchange of Information

Figure 7-1

After the confidentiality agreement has been signed, the parties then proceed to exchange basic information, including the following items.

- Historical financial statements
- Detailed organizational structures and ownership data
- A list of current projects and existing backlog
- A personnel roster (with salaries)
- An outline of employee benefits packages
- Long term liabilities of seller (i.e., bank financing and buy-out agreements)
- Details of professional liability insurance coverage
- Details of past or pending professional liability claims
- Information on any current space and equipment leases

Sometimes referred to as a "term sheet" or "memorandum of understanding," the letter of intent is the document that outlines the major points of the transaction. The primary topic of the letter of intent is a determination of the purchase price, although it should also establish the key terms of the deal, identify any other issues that will need to be addressed in the final agreement, and set conditions that must be met for the deal to go forward.

Within this framework, there are infinite variations in what the letter may contain. Some people distinguish between "binding" and "non-binding" letters of intent, although most of these letters are, in fact, a combination of the two— some paragraphs are binding and some are not. It's important that both parties agree beforehand on which sections will be binding— trouble often arises if the parties disagree on which items are binding and which are not. Like offers to buy property, these letters represent some kind of legal commitment, so they are generally (but not always) prepared by (or with advice from) attorneys.

Sometimes it's impossible to proceed as deliberately as a detailed letter of intent would suggest. In cases where interest in a particular seller is high, buyers must be prepared to make offers on more of a "bidding" basis. They will have to specify a price and structure, but should try to get an exclusive negotiation provision in return. Other highly sought-after sellers, particularly ones that have done their homework and talked to more than one potential buyer, may put up obstacles to signing a letter of intent. Buyers need to discriminate between the intractable seller (one who isn't really going to sell) and the seller who takes the transaction seriously, values his own time, and wants certain key terms settled before signing the letter. In the latter case, it can be much smoother sailing after the letter because much of the hard work has already been done.

The Process of Preparing the Letter of Intent

The process of preparing the letter of intent involves a coordinated effort among the internal team members and their lawyers and accountants. The attorneys structure the transaction from a corporate perspective and act as the primary negotiators. The tax attorney and the accountants work together to address the tax issues in the transaction. The intermediary's primary job is to keep the process moving forward, and in that role, must maintain good communication with all the principal players in order to help identify and resolve issues outside of the negotiating table. However, it is the principals of each firm who must continually maintain an open dialogue with each other. Each party must keep its goals and objectives for entering into the transaction in the forefront and be responsive to the goals and objectives of the other party. The principals of each firm must develop an ability to discuss the thorny issues which arise if they are to work together as a team after the closing.

Preparing the letter of intent begins with determining the substantive terms of the transaction, and the identifying potential "deal breakers" along the way. Part of the art of the deal is to resolve the deal breakers and agree upon a comprehensive letter of intent.

A form of letter of intent is shown in Appendix C.

Inside the Letter of Intent

As the parties to a proposed transaction begin to agree on the fundamental terms and conditions, the letter of intent becomes the vehicle for verifying and clarifying both parties' understanding of the essential terms of the proposed transaction. The process of preparing a letter of intent assists the parties in refining the terms of the proposed transaction or, in some instances, may reveal that the parties do not share a common view of the proposed transaction. Negotiating and preparing a letter of intent serves to bring out concerns which, if unaddressed and unresolved, might later develop into "deal breakers."

Letters of intent vary considerably in style and substance according to the nature and size of the proposed transaction and the functions the parties intend the letter of intent to serve. Generally, a letter of intent should be sufficiently detailed to

What Does the Letter of Intent Do?

Figure 7-2

The letter of intent is the document that outlines the major points of the transaction. The primary topic is a determination of the purchase price, although it should address all fundamental aspects of the deal.

The letter of intent is generally intended to do the following:

- Establish a basis for the purchase price
- Establish critical terms of the deal
- Identify issues that need further negotiation or consideration
- Summarize key financial and legal terms
- Serve as a basis for the buyer to secure necessary financing
- Guide conduct until closing or cut-off
- Guide subsequent negotiations
- Provide a basis for building consensus among interested parties

Good Intentions: A Look at the Letter of Intent

Figure 7-3

What's the intent of the letter of intent? Is it the "engagement ring" of the merger and acquisition process or not worth the paper it's written on? The answer is probably neither, but the letter of intent is still perhaps the most important step in a transaction. In short, the purpose of a letter of intent is to establish the key terms of the deal, to identify other issues that should be addressed in the final agreement, and to set conditions that must be met for the deal to go forward.

Within this framework, there are infinite variations in what the letter may contain. People distinguish between "binding" and "non-binding" letters of intent. However, most of these letters are in fact a combination of the two, with some paragraphs binding and some not. Trouble often arises from disagreements over which items are binding. Like offers to buy property, these letters represent some kind of legal commitment so they are generally, but not always, prepared by, or with advice from, attorneys.

Some people would like the letter of intent to resemble a purchase and sale agreement, spelling out details down to what kind of car the principals will drive and binding both parties to the deal. The trouble with a comprehensive and binding letter of intent is that neither buyer nor seller have enough information to completely know what they're getting into. Firms that skip the letter of intent or negotiate too detailed a letter may not have a higher failure rate, but they certainly waste more time.

The letter of intent should be the acid test for whether a potential deal exists. It should be sufficiently binding to give both parties the confidence to commit the time and money necessary to finalize the deal, but not so binding that either is afraid to go forward. The best letters are executed after the parties have gotten to know each other, discussed possible deal structures and deal-breakers, and reached consensus that a deal is workable and desirable. These are non-binding working statements that lay out the road map and schedule to the purchase and sale. Milestone dates keep both parties on track as the final agreement is developed.

Sometimes it's impossible to proceed as deliberately as this. In cases where interest in a particular seller is high, buyers must be prepared to make offers on more of a "bidding" basis. They will have to specify a price and structure, but should try to get an exclusive negotiation provision in return. Other highly sought-after sellers, particularly ones that have done their homework and talked to more than one potential buyer, may put up many obstacles to signing a letter of intent. Buyers need to discriminate between the intractable seller (who isn't really going to sell) and the seller who takes the transaction seriously, values his own time, and wants certain key terms settled before signing the letter. In the latter case, it can be much smoother sailing after the letter because the hard work has already been done.

Making an offer for anything is always a leap of faith. As usual, the best advice is to generate more than one possibility so you have options and aren't at the mercy of a single prospect. However, don't forget that some good things are worth waiting for.

satisfy both parties and their advisors that a deal does in fact exist, but it need not reflect the level of detail of a definitive acquisition agreement. The level of detail will be dictated by the complexity of the deal. It will also be affected by whether the parties wish to use it merely to confirm that there has been a "meeting of the minds" before they proceed, in a sense, using it as a road map for subsequent discussions and concluding the transaction. In any event, the letter of intent should be sufficiently flexible to permit the parties to vary the terms as the negotiations proceed.

Whatever the form, a letter of intent fulfills a number of purposes. It is primarily intended to:

- establish a basis for the purchase price; and
- give the parties some assurance that the critical terms of the deal have been agreed upon before they spend time and money to negotiate and prepare the final documentation, complete the due diligence review and consummate the closing.

It is also intended to:

- isolate difficult issues that will require further negotiation or consideration;
- summarize key financial and legal terms of the transaction which will serve as the basis for preparing definitive legal documents;
- provide the buyer with a preliminary document to be used as a basis for discussion with prospective lenders to line up any required financing;
- include binding provisions regarding the conduct of the parties until final documentation is in place or until the transaction has been abandoned (e.g., confidentiality provisions, provisions relating to the buyer's due diligence review, and "no shop" provisions); and
- guide and influence subsequent negotiations; and/or to provide a starting point for consensus building, especially if multiple parties (e.g. controlling stockholders, creditors, founders, etc.) will be required to approve the transaction.

Negotiating the Preliminary Purchase Price

During the negotiation of the purchase price, the value of the seller, and the form(s) of payment used by the buyer will have an impact on what each side thinks is a fair price.

Valuation of the Seller

The primary deal point in the preparation of a letter of intent is the determination of the purchase price and the terms of its payment. Included in the term "purchase price" is all consideration being paid, including payment for stock or assets, consulting/non-competition agreements and any bonuses that will be paid to the seller's principals.

There have been volumes written about the valuation process for A/E/P and environmental consulting firms. The literature on the subject uses book value, com-

Getting the Most For Your Firm

Figure 7-4

In actual transactions, it is not the case that factors like net revenues, operating profits, book value, backlog, and number of employees have equal weight when valuing a firm. Any good investor, financial analyst, or certified business appraiser will tell you that, bottom-line, the value of your firm is essentially the after-tax cash that can be put in your pocket. Buyers in the A/E/P and environmental consulting industries, however, seem to have a different perspective on how to evaluate the value of a firm.

Here are two extreme examples:

"The Bubble Will Burst" Theory for highly profitable firms. Suppose an engineering firm has had operating profits of at least twice the industry average for the last three years! You would think a buyer would be willing to pay a premium for such a successful company. However, the general thinking is that the firm won't be able to sustain its impressive profitability long-term. Potential buyers will guarantee only a portion of their proposed purchase price— the remainder is contingent on the firm's profitability continuing to exceed the industry average.

"Anything You Can Do I Can Do Better" Theory for firms losing money. On the other hand, suppose an engineering firm had operating losses last year and has basely been able to break even over the last several years. In this scenario, a buyer in our business believes that he knows a better way to operate the business. Rather than paying a low price for a firm with minimal (or zero) cash flow, he is willing to pay more than other potential buyers because he assumes he can cut costs, or increase revenues, and, therefore, increase the profitability of the firm.

Both theories encourage firm owners to focus on essentially one factor in increasing the value of their firm— build-up the firm's revenue in the short term, and sell the company to a buyer who is already working in our industry.

The problem is that you need more than revenues to survive. If the "white knight" buyer doesn't appear when you want (or need) it to, you could be left with a firm in disarray— high revenues, huge expenses, and no plan to fix the situation! But if you can create a strategic plan that has a specific schedule to build revenues and then find a buyer in advance of a potential crisis, you will probably maximize the value of your investment.

parative values, historical earnings trends, and various other criteria developing numerous valuation formulas. In addition, the seller often has intangible assets which must be factored into the equation. Such assets include market niche, backlog, location and staff strength.

Based on its own valuation at the beginning of the transaction process, the seller should have a good idea of the range of its value. To this should be added what the seller thinks the buyer perceives as valuable, such as location, market niche, and key employees.

If the deal involves an exchange of the buyer's stock for the assets or stock of the seller, then a valuation of the buyer is also necessary. In this situation, the exercise involves comparing the two values and arriving at a fair exchange rate; it is useful to use the same valuation formula for both the buyer and seller. If the stock of the buyer is publicly traded, then its value is easily ascertainable, although the parties must negotiate an appropriate adjustment if the stock price at the closing is outside of a previously agreed upon range.

Provisions for Payment

The letter of intent also lays out the terms for payment of the purchase price. The purchase price may be payable in full at the closing or in installments thereafter, either in a fixed amount or on a contingent basis. The letter should specify whether the buyer intends to acquire the stock of the target firm, or only certain assets.

A pricing scheme outline and payment schedule should also be included. The letter should state whether the consideration paid by the buyer will include cash,

Intangibles are Worth Consideration

Figure 7-5

Acquisitions occur for many reasons, but often, the buyer's main objective is to obtain the *intangible* assets that are not shown on any balance sheet. And for seller's, these intangibles can translate into big bucks. Four of the most strategic intangibles are:

Market niche— This may be the reason the target firm was picked in the first place. The price paid for a firm engaged in a growing or developing market (i.e., health care or infrastructure) will be higher than for firms operating in stagnant or declining markets (i.e., environmental labs or luxury hotels).

Backlog— Whenever someone can buy a firm with a nearly guaranteed cash flow from already existing work, the buyer will pay a premium. The immediate cost savings to the buyer who doesn't need to sink additional money into marketing costs to support his new acquisition makes the premium paid worthwhile.

Location— This criteria is not limited to the real estate industry. Strategic buying in burgeoning markets is a key impetus in mergers and acquisitions. Smart planners in the A/E/P and environmental consulting industries know where the future growth markets are, and pursue targets in those areas *before* they become hot markets.

Staff— Technical ability is important, but so is identifying who sells the work, who has a particular "following" of key clients, and so on. A buyer should be aware of the number of employees and their utilization rates, the professional-to-administrative staff ratio, and the ages of important staff members. A firm's value could drop if many of its shareholders and key personnel are approaching retirement age, not to mention the costs of engaging buy/sell agreements for shareholders who will be retiring a few years after the deal closes.

Are Earnouts a Good Idea?

Figure 7-6

It's only natural that the seller in an acquisition believes his firm is worth more than the buyer does. Many times, firms use "earnouts" to settle these differences of opinion. Earnouts are future payments to the seller in a deal, based on the ability of the combined firm to meet pre-determined criteria.

Ed Vick, chairman of 800-person consulting engineering firm **Kimley-Horn & Associates** (Raleigh, NC), advocates earnouts in certain situations. "They're an effective way of putting up the proof if a seller has one notion of the value of his firm, versus that of the person buying," he says. "It's also a way to keep the seller interested in the success of the ongoing entity."

There are generally three kinds of earnouts: profit-based, revenue-based, and performance-based. Each comes with its own benefits and drawbacks.

Profit-based earnouts can be disadvantageous to the seller because profits are often hard to define. The buying firm can also manipulate the numbers, reducing the rewards to the seller.

Dames & Moore (Los Angeles, CA), a 5,300-employee environmental consulting firm, uses profit-based earnouts in many of its deals, according to Bob Perry, executive vice president. But the firm attempts to avoid trouble by carefully and precisely defining the criteria that will be used to determine the earnout, and including that information in its closing documents.

Revenue-based earnouts can be a disadvantage to the buyer because it may serve as an incentive for the seller to take on low profit work. They can also be confusing to both parties because, when the project revenues are mixed within the firm after the sale, credit can be hard to determine. This may discourage the smooth integration of the acquired firm.

"We steer clear of that," says Vick. "It encourages volume without regard for profit." Vick says a firm determined to use this form of earnout could base the revenue figure on a set multiplier, preventing the seller from taking on low-multiplier work to boost the revenue figures. "It needs to be based on *earned* revenue," he says.

Performance-based earnouts present the same problem that many firms face when attempting to set fair compensation for employees— what are the standards?

Kimley-Horn uses performance-based earnouts, Vick says, because the firm already has a system in place that rewards employees based on their individual performance, as well as on the performance of the firm as a whole. "I think that it would be very hard to do if a firm didn't have a system in place," says Vick. "Establishing a set of rules specifically for the seller would be a problem. If you have a performance-based incentive compensation system in place, it's a lot easier to implement in a transaction."

The point: the spirit of the deal is critical. Both buyer and seller must share risks and rewards. If one group goes in feeling they got the worst of deal, they're certain to get their revenge.

stock, notes, all three, or some combination. An approximate figure to be paid should be determined, along with the basis for that price (e.g. accrual book value at a specified date, or specific assets at some value and accounts receivable that are less than 90 days old). The payment schedule should specify how much will be paid at the closing and if needed, what the installment payment schedule will be.

It's only natural that the seller in an acquisition will believe his firm is worth more than the buyer does, and many times firms use "earnouts" to settle these differences. Earnouts are future payments made to the seller in a deal, based on the ability of the combined firm to meet pre-determined criteria. Earnouts allow the seller to prove the firm's stated value, and keep the seller interested in the ongoing success of the entity after the closing.

There are generally three basic types of earnouts, namely profit-based earnouts, revenue-based earnouts, and performance-based earnouts:

- ***Profit-based Earnouts.*** Profit-based earnouts can be disadvantageous to the seller because profits are often hard to define. There is potential for the buying firm to manipulate the number, reducing the rewards to the seller. Firms can avoid trouble by carefully and precisely defining the criteria that will be used to determine the earnout, and setting forth the components of the profit-and-loss statement (which are used to calculate the profit) in the closing documents.

- ***Revenue-based Earnouts.*** Revenue-based earnouts can be a disadvantage to the buyer because they may serve as an incentive for the seller to take on all work, even if the profit margin is low. The buyer will want to take steps to ensure that the revenue is adjusted to take into account low margin volume. Revenue-based earnouts can also be confusing to both parties because, when the project revenues are mixed with the firm after the sale, credit can be hard to determine. This may even discourage the smooth integration of the acquired firm.

- ***Performance-based Earnouts.*** This form of earnout is based on the performance of the individual as well as the performance of the firm as a whole. Performance-based earnouts present the same problem that many firms face when attempting to set fair compensation for employees— what are the standards? Performance-based earnouts are a lot easier to implement in a transaction if you already have a performance-based compensation system in place.

In any case, each party must view the terms of the earnout as fair to both parties in the transaction. The spirit of the deal is critical. Both the buyer and the seller must share risks and rewards. If one group goes in feeling they got the worst of the deal, they're certain to look for revenge. The details of any contingency payments should be clearly defined in the letter of intent (e.g. operating profits vs. pre-bonus profits versus pre-corporate allocation profits), and any reductions due to missed criteria should be fully explained.

Provisions of the Letter of Intent

Letters of intent typically contain both a binding contract and non-binding provisions. The non-binding provisions typically relate to the terms and conditions of the proposed transaction, and the binding provisions typically relate to the conduct of the parties between the signing of the letter of intent and the signing of a definitive acquisition agreement. It is extremely important that the express language of the letter of intent make it absolutely clear which provisions are intended to be legal obligations and which provisions are intended to be non-binding. This is usually accomplished by including a clear statement at the beginning or end of the letter of intent:

"This letter is intended to express ABC, Inc.'s intent with respect to the purchase of XYZ Corporation and it is expressly agreed and understood that, with the limited exception of paragraphs 2,5,6 and 17 which shall be legally binding on the parties from and after the execution of this letter, this letter does not constitute an enforceable agreement, is not legally binding upon any of the parties hereto and imposes no duty or obligation on any of them to proceed with the transactions discussed herein."

Another approach is to divide the letter of intent into sections, each of which has a preamble that indicates whether it is intended to bind the parties.

A third approach, which offers the flexibility of creating a non-binding working statement of present intention and provides a structure for imposing clear and en-

Outline of Binding and Non-Binding Provisions Figure 7-7

The letter of intent includes both binding and non-binding provisions, which usually include the following:

Binding Provisions

- Confidentiality
- Access
- Good Faith Negotiation
- Public Announcements
- Expenses and Termination
- No-Shop Clause

Non-Binding Provisions

- Subject Matter and Structure
- Purchase Price
- Liabilities
- Accounts Receivable
- Employee Agreements
- Representations and Warranties
- Indemnification
- Conditions to Closing
- Closing

forceable obligations, is the use of a separate binding agreement. The agreement acknowledges the execution of a non-binding letter of intent, recites consideration, and contains all of the obligations which the parties want to be binding and enforceable on each other. This avoids the hybrid "yes I am, no I'm not" binding/non-binding letter of intent, which sometimes causes ambiguity and can create problems.

Legally Binding Provisions

Provisions that are typically included as "legally binding" elements of a letter of intent are access (for due diligence purposes), good faith negotiation, public announcements, expenses and termination, and the no-shop clause.

Access

The buyer will want the contractual right of access to the seller's place of business, books and records for the purpose of conducting its due diligence review. The seller's concerns are that the investigation not unduly disrupt its business and that the buyer will keep all proprietary information confidential. The first of these concerns is typically addressed in the access provision itself with language to the effect that the investigation will be performed during customary business hours and in such a manner as not to disrupt the seller's business. The second of these concerns is dealt with in a separate provision or a separate agreement concerning confidentiality. Oftentimes a separate confidentiality agreement is entered into before the letter of intent is drafted. This is usually the case when there is preliminary due diligence performed prior to the execution of the letter of intent.

The issue of when the seller wants its employees and clients to know about the proposed sale of the business can impact the access given to the buyer. Often the seller is concerned that widespread knowledge about the proposed sale could adversely affect business, and will want to limit the buyer's contact with these people until it has a fairly high level of assurance that the deal will go through. In this situation, the seller may even require that the buyer defer its due diligence investigation until a definitive acquisition agreement has been signed. Should this be the case, the buyer should ensure that the agreement includes clear "outs" in the event of unsatisfactory findings.

Good Faith Negotiation

Sometimes letters of intent include binding provisions stating that the parties will "negotiate in good faith and use their best efforts to arrive at a mutually acceptable definitive agreement." Each party should consider carefully whether it wants such a provision. Basically, this provision gives the party seeking to force the consummation of a transaction an additional argument that can ultimately be raised in court and used to threaten the other party. As a general rule, if either party believes itself to be at a disadvantage or that it may be at a disadvantage after the signing of the letter of intent and before the signing of the definitive agreement, it may want that provision.

Public Announcements

Many letters of intent include a provision requiring the prior approval of both parties regarding the timing and content of all public announcements. These provisions are aimed at facilitating the process and are not usually controversial.

War Story: Planning for Public Announcements

Figure 7-8

WHEN A MERGER or acquisition seems imminent and you are ready to release information to the press, make sure the firm you are dealing with knows what you're doing— one way to do this is to address public announcements in the letter of intent. In some instances, an uncontrolled quest for PR can cause a sure thing to go south in a hurry because either the buyer or the seller is not ready to make an announcement.

Recently a potential merger collapsed, in part because one of the parties talked to the press without the consent of the other. Two architectural firms in the Southeast had all but signed on the dotted line, according to a principal in one of the firms. He couldn't wait to get the word out and spoke frankly with a reporter from a local paper. What started out as a sure thing turned into a dead end, however— shortly after the buyer told the local newspaper that a deal had been struck, the other party reported that the deal was dead.

So no matter how eager you are to get PR for a merger or acquisition deal, make sure the other party is ready to see its name in print before you talk to the press.

Nevertheless, the interests of the buyer and the seller with regard to public announcements may differ in some instances. For example, the seller may wish to make a public announcement as early as possible to encourage other bidders, and the buyer may wish to delay announcement as long as possible to avoid an auction. Alternatively, the seller may be concerned that a public announcement might adversely impact its business and may therefore wish to delay such an announcement as long as possible, whereas the buyer may wish to make a public announcement of the transaction as early as possible in order to give it additional leverage in subsequent negotiations of the definitive agreement and make it more difficult for the seller to abandon the transaction. This issue of how and when to make a public announcement is always a difficult topic. At some point, clients and employees will have to be told of the transaction. The later the announcement, the more confidentiality that is assured. However, postponing the announcement can result in heightened anxiety among employees of seller.

Of course, it is possible to negotiate limitations on the timing of a public announcement. If such restrictions are negotiated, they should contain an overriding right on the part of either party to make public disclosure if that party is advised by counsel that disclosure is required by law. When a transaction involves one or more public companies, and the transaction is material to one or more of the public companies, federal securities laws require that public announcement of the pending transaction must be made at that point in the discussions when the transaction is sufficiently probable that a reasonable investor would consider it significant in making decisions regarding his or her investment in the company's stock.

Expenses and Termination

Typically, letters of intent contain provisions stating that each of the parties will bear its own expenses or describing the agreement the parties may have made with regard to expenses. Letters of intent should also have termination provisions which provide that if by a certain date a definitive agreement has not been entered into, the letter terminates and the parties are released from their obligations and understandings. This provision should not apply to the confidentiality and noncompetition provisions, which should survive the termination of the letter of intent.

Neither side should be obligated to continue talks forever. A reasonable time frame for signing the letter of intent as well as for signing a formal binding purchase agreement should be carefully negotiated and clearly stated. This is usually in the 90- to 180-day range, and if a purchase agreement is not signed within this time, all bets are off.

The No-Shop Clause

The basic purpose of a no-shop clause is to require the seller to take its business off the market or to otherwise limit the seller's right to solicit or accept other offers for a certain defined period while the buyer conducts its due diligence and the parties negotiate. Buyers consider this type of provision very important for a number of reasons. First, the buyer does not want to be involved in a bidding contest. In addition, the buyer wants to avoid a situation where it proceeds with due diligence, retains lawyers and accountants to assist with the transaction, and perhaps pays commitment fees to financing sources, only to find that the seller has accepted an offer from another party. The scope of a no-shop clause can range from a so-called lockup, in which the seller makes a broad agreement not to consider or accept other offers, to a more limited agreement by the seller not to solicit other offers. Sometimes other mechanisms, such as right of first refusal options (which give the party the opportunity to match any other offer), break-up fees (which are paid to the buyer if the seller does not go through with the transaction), and topping fees (which are paid to the buyer should another firm make a better offer), are used to protect against other offers.

War Story: The Earlier-Than-Planned Public Announcement

Figure 7-9

A MIDWESTERN consulting engineering firm was considering acquiring a smaller firm in another state that was facing internal management issues. During the due diligence phase, the acquiring firm's management consultant determined that staff members in the target firm were apprehensive about the stability of their firm, the rumor mill was generating stories of an outside sale, and as a result, many of them were considering other employment opportunities. Management of the acquiring firm assessed the situation and decided to make an earlier-than-planned announcement of their intentions. In presenting their plans to the staff of the target firm, they allayed the employees fears, got them pumped up about the future of the company, and brought stability to the situation, allowing the due diligence process to continue.

In circumstances where the seller is a publicly-held company (or a private company with too many stockholders to make it practical for the seller to obtain stockholder approval prior to agreeing to a no-shop provision) the decision by the seller's board of directors to agree to a no-shop provision is subject to the directors' fiduciary duties under state law. Under these circumstances, the seller may argue that it is unable to agree to a no-shop provision, or that any no-shop provision must be limited in scope and contain broad "fiduciary outs." If the seller takes such a position, the buyer must be knowledgeable about the relevant rules imposed on directors by the seller's state of incorporation in order to be able to negotiate the broadest possible no-shop provision that will be enforceable under the relevant state law.

The buyer should try to draft the "fiduciary out" narrowly, to the effect that the seller will not solicit any offers for, or participate in any discussions or negotiations, or furnish any information to anyone with respect to a sale, merger, or other disposition of the business of the seller or any part thereof, subject only to the fiduciary duty of the directors under applicable law, as advised in writing by counsel. This type of language would give the buyer the maximum possible security.

Non-Binding Provisions

Though the subject matter and structure of letters of intent are as varied as the transactions they describe, certain provisions are commonly featured in almost all letters of intent. The basic non-binding provisions that are typically included are subject matter and structure, purchase price, liabilities, accounts receivable, employee agreements, representations and warrantees, indemnification, closing, and conditions to closing.

Subject Matter and Structure

The letter of intent should describe what is to be acquired (i.e., stock, assets or contract rights), and should identify, to the extent it is known, the proposed structure of the transaction (i.e., whether it is to be a purchase, a merger, or a consolidation).

Purchase Price

Both the purchase price and the manner of payment should be clearly stated in the letter of intent. To the extent that the amount payable is contingent (either in whole or in part) on future events or financial results, the formula for calculating the amount of such payments should be clearly defined. In addition, it is advisable to identify who has the final authority to determine the amount of the payment due. It is also not uncommon to provide a mechanism for the resolution of disputes. Factors that may either increase or decrease the purchase price to be paid, and the method of calculating any adjustment should be outlined in detail.

In the event of payment by promissory note, the letter of intent should set forth the principal amount of the note, the term of the note, the rate at which interest will accrue under the note, the security, if any, for the payment of the note, the terms, if any, on which the note is to be subordinated to other indebtedness of the buyer, and any rights of offset that the maker of the note may have. The parties should also state whether the note is to be considered negotiable or non-negotiable.

If payment is to be made in stock, the letter of intent should set forth either the number of shares to be tendered, or the valuation method for determining the number of shares to be tendered. If the stock is restricted and/or unregistered, the parties may wish to include provisions relating to either demand or piggy-back registration rights (technical securities issues).

With respect to payment in property (as opposed to cash, notes or securities) careful consideration should be given to the method of valuing such property and to the inclusion of necessary representations and warranties as to the condition or value of such property.

Liabilities

The letter of intent should express clearly the liabilities to be assumed by the buyer and the liabilities to be retained by the seller. The parties may also wish to make specific provisions for items of particular concern, such as the treatment of uninsured liabilities, professional liability claims and the like.

Accounts Receivable

The letter of intent in an acquisition of assets should clearly state whether accounts receivable are included in the assets being acquired. If the accounts receivable are being retained by the seller, the buyer may wish to include language on the methods of collection that may be employed by seller. If the accounts receivable are being acquired by the buyer, the buyer may wish to include language requiring a guarantee by seller of collectibility.

Typical Conditions to Closing

Figure 7-10

All letters of intent should include a statement of the conditions to either party's obligation to consummate the proposed transaction.

The following are typical conditions to closing:

- Negotiation, execution, and delivery of a definitive acquisition agreement
- Approval of the board of directors of the buyer/seller
- Approval of the seller's stockholders
- Approval of the buyer's/seller's lenders
- Attainment of financing for the buyer
- Receipt of necessary consents of third parties and governmental entities
- Execution of employment contracts and non-competition agreements
- Satisfactory completion of the buyer's due diligence review
- No material adverse change in the condition, business, operations, or prospects of the firm to be acquired (or buyer if stock is used as consideration)

Employment, Consulting, and Non-Competition Agreements

A letter of intent will frequently include provisions relating to employment, consulting, or non-competition agreements that must either be offered to or obtained from employees of the seller. The buyer may wish to include a provision requiring particular employees or affiliated companies to enter into covenants not to compete, the essential terms of which may either be articulated in the letter of intent or reserved for a subsequent negotiation.

Representations and Warranties

The letter of intent may specify particular representations and warranties to be made in connection with the proposed transaction, or in lieu of this approach, may include a statement that the definitive agreement will include representations and warranties that are "usual and customary in a transaction of this type" or, if the buyer wishes to exercise greater control, "are satisfactory to the buyer."

Indemnification

It is not uncommon for the letter of intent to identify the issues for which indemnification will be provided and to set forth upper and lower monetary limits (i.e., the cap and basket) on the seller's (and/or seller's stockholders) obligation to secure the buyer from loss or legal responsibility. Letters of intent frequently also include very specific indemnification provisions with respect to known liabilities.

Closing

The letter of intent will usually set forth a date of closing, and provide that the parties may agree to a later date. If the letter of intent includes a binding "no-shop" provision, it is customary to also include a "drop dead" date, at which time the transaction will be deemed to have been abandoned.

Conditions to Closing

All letters of intent should include a statement of the conditions to either party's obligation to consummate the proposed transaction. Some typical provisions include:

- negotiation, execution and delivery of a definitive acquisition agreement;
- approval of the buyer's/seller's board of directors;
- approval of seller's stockholders;
- approval of the buyer's/seller's lenders;
- attainment of financing (buyer);
- receipt of the necessary consents of third parties and governmental entities;
- execution of employment contracts and non-competition agreements;

- satisfactory completion of the buyer's due diligence review (usually by a date specified); and
- no material adverse change in the condition, business, operations, or prospects of the firm to be acquired.

Omitting the Letter of Intent

In some instances, parties elect to omit the letter of intent and proceed directly to the preparation of final documentation. This approach can save time and expense in situations where both parties are comfortable that they both understand and agree on the important terms of the transaction. More often than not, however, omitting the letter of intent results in the process being more time consuming and costly when major issues arise after the drafting has commenced.

Conclusion

The letter of intent outlines the major points of the transaction, and should be the acid test for whether a potential deal exists. It should be sufficiently binding to give both parties the confidence to commit the time and money necessary to finalize the deal, but not so binding that either is afraid to go forward. The best letters are executed after the parties have gotten to know each other, discussed possible deal structures and deal breakers, and reached consensus that a deal is both workable and desirable. The letter is basically a series of working statements that lay out the road map and schedule to the purchase and sale. Milestone dates will keep both parties on track as the final agreement is developed.

Once the letter of intent has been signed, both parties can move full steam ahead into the due diligence process. Chapter 8 will explain more about due diligence, including what it is supposed to accomplish and how to proceed in a systematic manner that will yield the greatest results in the least amount of time.

8 The Due Diligence Investigation

The Due Diligence Investigation

☑ *Gathering information as part of conducting due diligence gives both parties a chance to investigate the details of each other's operations. The goal of conducting a due diligence investigation is to identify issues of concern before the transaction takes place.*

Introduction

Due diligence is one of the most tedious and painstaking tasks associated with a merger or acquisition, but it is also one of the most important. If you're dreading the due diligence investigation, remind yourself that you are trying to uncover issues that could turn into nightmares if you don't find out about them until after the transaction has taken place.

Knowing a little about the due diligence process can help you be better prepared for this stage in the transaction, and having a plan for collecting and reviewing information can make the task a little less daunting, but if you're still dreading it, maybe you should consider hiring a consulting firm to conduct the due diligence investigation for you. An outside firm is likely to have the resources and experience necessary to get the job done quickly and thoroughly, allow you to concentrate on other aspects of the transaction, and make objective, impartial observations and analyses.

The first order of business is to decide who will be in charge of conducting the investigation. Will it be a team of your internal and external advisors, or will you hire an outside firm? Next you should consider and plan for how the task will be managed, especially if it will be managed internally. Who will be responsible for getting what information? The orderly collection and review of information can make the research much simpler.

It also helps to know what the goals of the due diligence investigation are for both the buyer and the seller. There are a number of tangible results you can expect to come from the inquiry, and knowing how to put those results to work for you will makes the whole process well worth the time and energy you expend.

Defining Due Diligence

The phrase "due diligence" refers to the process whose principal objective is to obtain, review, and understand all relevant information about the transaction partner. It's a mistake to think of due diligence as simply sending your accountants in to confirm financial matters. Experienced buyers know that qualitative measures (such as competitive factors and management team capabilities) are just as critical as the quantitative measures.

The process begins with the first information you receive regarding your prospective transaction partner— at which point it is usually referred to as "preliminary due diligence." The investigation reaches its greatest intensity, however, once the

War Story: Negotiating a Deal

Figure 8-1

ACQUIRING A FIRM can be a frustrating, costly experience with no guarantee of success. But the right decisions during negotiations, especially the final "due diligence" phase, can make the difference between a prime acquisition and a dud. Acquisition veterans agree principals must, above all else, avoid talking themselves into a bad deal.

When **Trow Consulting Engineers Ltd.** (Brampton, ON), a 400-person firm, was negotiating with a small engineering firm in the Chicago area a few years ago, Trow president Chris Thompson found the selling principal "picky." Despite that and other minor misgivings, Thompson went ahead with the deal. It was a disaster. Thompson says they ignored one of the most dangerous warning signs in an acquisition: *incompatibility* apparent at the negotiating table.

Irv Weiss, president of **Pickering, Inc.** (Memphis, TN), a 150-person environmental firm, says principals sometimes concentrate on the positives of a potential acquisition and are blind to the negatives. "You're love-struck because you found some apparent qualities or characteristics you need in an acquisition, so you may be tempted to ignore items that come up during the due diligence phase," he says.

Principals experienced in acquisitions warn not to overlook anything during due diligence— the last step of the process is as important as the first.

parties have agreed to the conditions spelled out in the letter of intent. The letter of intent will often include a clause pertaining to due diligence access, and the signing of the letter serves as the kickoff for the formal information-gathering process. The length of the investigation varies in every case, but you should plan to complete your research prior to preparing and executing definitive transaction documents such as the purchase and sale agreement.

Knowing where to look for information about your transaction partner can make sure that you cover all the bases. You shouldn't worry about asking too many questions— remember that what you don't uncover now has the potential come back to haunt you later. Be creative about where you look for information, too, because facts about your transaction partner will come from many different sources. For example, you can collect marketing materials that the firm sends out to clients. Have discussions with all of the firm's principals and with employees at every level. Request information from credit reporting bureaus, and question your partner about any problems that turn up. Survey past and present clients about the work the firm has done, and look to the clients of competitors to find out why they do not work with the firm you are investigating. Trade organizations and other industry professionals can often testify as to the reputation of the firm within the profession, and you can always check to see if the firm has ever been written up or had a project reviewed by a trade publication. Keep in mind throughout that the due diligence process seeks to develop a profile of *all* aspects of your transaction partner.

The Due Diligence Team

The due diligence investigation serves as the means of confirming any assumptions that you may have made about the other firm. Approach the investigation in an efficient and comprehensive manner to be sure that no topic is overlooked, that unnecessary effort is not expended, and that the inquiry results will be useful. If you don't hire an outside firm to conduct the investigation for you, your best bet is to carefully assemble your due diligence team and outline which matters each group on your team will address. If every person knows their role and the goals of the process, a coordinated effort can yield tremendous results.

M&A Attorney

The buyer's attorney (or management consultant) will usually prepare and distribute a general, comprehensive due diligence checklist to guide the investigation. Ultimately, the attorney is responsible for assembling the schedules and exhibits which will list the results of the due diligence investigation and be attached to the transaction documents. The M&A attorneys for both the buyer and seller also review and analyze any information identified in the due diligence process which may be problematic. They should quantify any problems, confer with the client, and ultimately negotiate its treatment or resolution in the transaction documents.

Assembling the information relating to legal matters such as corporate structure and organization, lawsuits and claims, retirement plan matters, and leases, is also the responsibility of the attorney. As the leader of the investigation, attorneys will usually call on someone from their office, sometimes a junior lawyer, to be responsible for inventorying and assembling all of the information that is gathered.

Accountant

As you might expect, accountants are generally concerned with reviewing the other party's financial information including historical financial statements (balance sheet, income statements, and sources of uses of funds), corporate tax returns, profit analyses (both generally and on a project-by-project basis), and a historical breakdown of revenues per client.

Management Consultant

In addition to assisting a firm with a search for a transaction partner, a management consultant can be retained to perform a number (but not all) of the tasks assigned to the M&A attorney and the accountant. Management consultants often specialize in preparing comprehensive due diligence reports, and they are able to conduct a due diligence investigation without having to tie up members of the firm's internal team. Any problematic information that is uncovered during the investigation can be further researched and analyzed by the consultant, and then presented to the firm with recommendations on how to handle the information. Schedules and exhibits to the transaction documents which list the results of the due diligence investigation can also be assembled by the consultant, and then turned over to the M&A attorney.

Management consultants are also able to review the other party's financial information, and provide a full report on the financial health of your transaction partner.

Hiring a management consultant as an advisor is an especially good choice for sellers, because the consultant has no ulterior interest in keeping the seller as a client. Other advisors to the seller face the prospect of losing a client if the deal goes through— a management consultant will not have a conflict of interest in analyzing the information and giving recommendations.

Professional Liability Insurance Consultant

Your professional liability insurance consultant should review existing insurance coverage, and take special note of exceptions and deductibles, current and past claims and losses, possible future claims, and the terms of coverage which will be appropriate after the closing.

The Internal Team

Your internal due diligence team should include senior staff members from human resources, operations, financial management and accounting, and management information systems. The members of the internal team are responsible for learning everything about their area of responsibility in the partner firm, and identifying issues which may come up later when the two firms begin the integration process.

The due diligence goals of buyers and sellers are similar in most aspects, but the form of the transaction will dictate which matters are of more concern to which party. A word of caution to those in charge: be sure to investigate thoroughly and take the time necessary to sufficiently complete the inquiry. There are a myriad of topics set forth in the due diligence checklist, and you need prepare the troops for a long and tedious process if you're going to get all of the information you need to make the investigation a success.

Special Due Diligence Considerations

When conducting due diligence, the parties should conduct their investigation according to whether the deal will be a transfer of assets or stock, and whether the transaction will be taxable or non-taxable.

Asset Transfer

In an asset transfer, the buyer purchases only certain specified tangible and/or intangible assets, and therefore can focus on evaluating the status of only the ongoing contracts it will assume after transaction. In addition, since many of the seller's employees may be terminated, the buyer should review the employees that the firm might re-hire. Most importantly, the sale of assets can usually be authorized by a majority or supermajority of the seller's stockholders, which should reduce the buyer's concern for obtaining a unanimous approval.

Stock Transfer

In transactions where there is a transfer of stock, the buyer legally assumes all of the seller's liabilities. In this case, the buyer should focus on collecting information regarding all such obligations, including accounts payable and accruals, vacation and sick time. Since accounts receivable are being purchased, a comprehensive understanding of aging, collectability issues, and reserves should also be addressed.

"Hot" and "Cold" Prospects

Figure 8-2

If you're thinking about buying a firm, be sure you recognize the differences between a "hot" and a "cold" prospect. A "hot" prospect is a firm already on the market, or one where the owners are actively trying to sell the firm. A "cold" prospect is a firm that is not on the market.

While the firms may appear similar, and differences may be subtle, thorough due diligence becomes increasingly important if you pursue a deal with a "hot" prospect. There is a potential for problems if your due diligence reveals any of the following about a firm actively on the market:

- If the owner has not been aggressive in collections or has accepted unfair price reduction requests made by clients, there may be hidden cash flow issues.
- If ongoing projects have been milked for profits, or if cash for marketing efforts has been limited, the company is likely in a defensive position.
- If the owners have been extracting critical capital assets or limiting investments in equipment, make sure you're getting everything you pay for in terms of long-term assets— after all, you don't normally put new tires on a car just before trading it in.
- If there are problems with clients or projects, or impending issues of liability, there may be other reasons for the sale.
- If the staff appears underpaid, it may be due to the owners' plan to sell the firm. Or if the staff appears overpaid, it may be to keep them from leaving before the impending sale. Either of these situations indicate that there are staff problems which will need to be resolved after the deal.
- If employees are nervous about the sale, they are likely involved in self-preservation activities— seeking another job, dragging work out, or positioning to appear important to prospective new owners. In addition, productivity may be lost due to rumors concerning the impending sale.

Project management, quality issues, or other aspects of good management may have been ignored.

A cold acquisition, on the other hand, may reduce the likelihood that these problems will occur, because the firm will be concentrating on continuing operations and looking further along the business horizon. Owners will have invested time and effort into ongoing business operations, and the general health of the firm should be better.

Finally, if you've identified a cold target, you've probably done your homework to identify the likelihood of a compatible match even before you contact the target firm. That, along with careful and sufficient due diligence, will significantly reduce the chances of a surprise after the deal is done.

*George L. Reed, J.D., P.E., is vice president in the Tallahassee office of 1,200-person consulting engineering firm **URS Consultants** (San Francisco, CA).*

Taxable and Nontaxable Transactions

Whether the transaction is an asset sale or a stock sale, the form of consideration will dictate the concerns of the seller and its principals. If the buyer is paying in cash, then the seller is not concerned with any risk in collecting the purchase price. On the other hand, if the buyer is paying in notes or stock, then the seller needs to focus on several additional issues. If notes are part of the purchase, then the seller needs to investigate the buyer's financial strength. Unless the obligation is secured by collateral, the seller should look for indicators that the buyer will be able to pay the deferred component at a later time. If the buyer's stock is part of the purchase, then the seller needs to have some confirmation of its value. The seller's stockholders must look into the provisions of the buyer's stock repurchase agreement, and the buyer's philosophy on stock ownership.

The Due Diligence Investigation

Being thorough is the key to a successful transaction. And the best way to make sure that your team conducts a comprehensive search that will yield the information you are looking for is to carefully plan out the areas and particular documents that need to be reviewed. A due diligence investigation checklist is included as Appendix D, but let's take a look at what kind of information you should look for in each of the areas.

Organization and Good Standing

Is the transaction partner registered with the appropriate professional boards regulating design professionals in states where it does business? Typically, each state also requires that the firm file a state income tax return and register as a foreign corporation doing business in the state. Is the firm in corporate good standing, with its minutebook and stockbook in order?

Capitalization and Stockholders/Authorization

Who owns or controls the stock of the transaction partner? Researchers should make a list of shareholders including the position, title, and percentage of ownership of each. Are there any stockholders who are not employees of the firm? Buyers will naturally be concerned with identifying those persons or entities whose consent is necessary for approving the transaction, or conversely, who can veto the transaction. Any buyouts in progress should be described and quantified.

Financial Statements and Tax Matters

The buyer must understand the historical financial performance (income statement) and balance sheet of the seller. What is the quality of the statements? Have they been compiled? reviewed? audited? Important financial indicators include gross margin, operating costs and profits, debt-to-equity and return-on-equity ratios, and direct vs. indirect labor totals (including a determination of multipliers, chargeability, and overhead rates). Positive or negative return on investment should also be noted, in addition to the salaries and bonuses of the shareholders, the markup on reimbursable expenses, and whether the accounting is done on a cash or accrual basis.

Backlog should be analyzed by compiling a list of major backlog clients and the contract amount of each. Of additional concern to the buyer is an in-depth understanding of work-in-progress, and the fees charged and paid to date compared to the percentage of the project completed to date. This information allows buyers to determine any future shortfall in billings.

Tax returns should be reviewed along with the most recent federal and state tax audits. The buyer needs to focus on the profits or losses recorded, in addition to finding issues which may impact the future financial performance of the seller, such as aggressive deductions of expenditures or the failure to take corrective action with regard to problems identified in previous audits.

Aged accounts receivable should be examined, including a list of clients and their respective amounts outstanding.

Staff Overview

A roster listing the name, title, function, exempt or non-exempt status, salary or hourly rate, and date of hire of each employee should be reviewed. The number of part-time and full-time employees should also be noted.

Employee Benefit Plans and Salary Labor Disputes

The list of the seller's employees and their respective salaries should be compared with the compensation levels of comparable employees in the buyer's firm. Are there any management or employment agreements? An important focus of any due diligence inquiry is a complete review of the details of benefit plans provided for the employees of the other party. A list of benefits should be made, listing the details for life, short-term and long-term disability, medical, and dental insurance, paid holidays and sick days, vacation, 401(k) and profit sharing plans, educational assistance, seminar reimbursement, and any other benefits the company offers. Any ESOP or stock bonus/option plans and retirement plans in existence should also be analyzed.

Other Contracts and Commitments

Most A/E/P and environmental consulting firms have some arrangement with a financial institution that includes a revolving credit line and/or term notes. Are any principals guarantors of such loans? What are the operating covenants in these agreements? Are the loans secured by assets of the firm or by individual assets? Employment agreements and offers of employment should also be reviewed, and any unusual information should be noted. Details of any severance packages should be included.

There are an unlimited number of types of contracts which may fall under into this category. It is necessary to review and understand each of them in order to accurately evaluate the commitments of the firm.

Leases

Most firms have several leases for office space or storage space. How does the rent compare to current market conditions? Leases for personal property such as equipment, computers and automobiles are also relevant. Information gathered should include the location and a description of all leased spaces, including the history and current terms of the lease, the general condition and appearance of the space, and notations on any problems or unused space.

Licenses

Are there sufficient licenses to cover the number of copies of software being used by the firm?

Professional Liability Insurance

A key element to any transaction is the orderly transition of professional liability coverage, an issue which is often not adequately investigated in the due diligence process. Which policy will cover the prior acts of the seller? Will the seller indemnify the buyer for the deductible which must be paid for any claims relating to prior acts? (This topic will be addressed in more depth later in this chapter.)

Other Insurance

Does the company have company, life or disability insurance on any of the principals or other employees? If so, note the details of the kind of coverage, policy amount, or unusual circumstances of each policy.

Litigation

All past and pending litigation claims must be thoroughly reviewed. Which claims are being defended by insurance carriers? Have the applicable deductibles been exhausted?

Patents and Trademarks

Have names, trademarks and other logos or service marks been registered, and are they protected?

Real Property

Often design firms are tenants in buildings owned by one or more of the principals. Is the real property to be included in the transaction? If so, refer to the checklist in Appendix D for a road map through the minefield of real estate and environmental issues which may arise.

Government Regulations/Environmental

Depending on the nature of the disciplines and services provided by the seller, compliance with the long list of rules and regulations may need to be reviewed.

Client Lists

A list of the seller's top 10 clients (in terms of billing) for the past two years, including firm name, the yearly fees, and percentage of total fees for each should be compiled and reviewed. An historical breakdown of revenue by client and market may also be helpful. The buyer will want to measure whether the seller is over-dependent on any client or market. Many seasoned buyers (or a professional third party) will interview the seller's key clients to determine whether such clients are well-served and satisfied, and to get a sense of how the client would react to a transaction.

Components of the Due Diligence Investigation

Figure 8-3

Due diligence is much more than just sending your accountant in to confirm financial matters. Your due diligence investigation should gathering information that pertains to the following areas:

- Organization and Good Standing
- Capitalization and Shareholders Authorization
- Financial Statements and Tax Matters
- Employee Benefit Plans and Salary Labor Disputes
- Other Contracts and Commitments
- Leases
- Licenses
- Professional Liability Insurance
- Other Insurance
- Litigation
- Patents and Trademarks
- Real Property
- Government Regulations/Environmental
- Client Lists
- Culture
- History and Ownership
- Leadership and Corporate Governance
- Personnel
- Quality of Services
- Organizational Chart

Professional Liability Insurance

Investigating the history and status of professional liability insurance is an area that is consistently overlooked in due diligence investigations— don't make this mistake. If a buyer fails to properly examine the claims history of a seller, then a significant portion of the picture will be missing when the buyer later tries to decide on a comprehensive insurance program that will cover the combined entity. Any unfavorable information that is uncovered should be fully explored by the buyer as potential evidence of poor management or inattention to professional standards on the part of the seller.

The buyer and the seller have different concerns regarding the insurability of professional liability claims related to professional services performed prior to and after the effective date of the transaction.

Seller's Issues

The seller's primary focus is to fully insure itself and its individual principals and employees against claims generated by its acts and services relating to the period prior to the transaction. It does not want to have any gaps in coverage. The coverage should be as broad as possible, providing a prudent deductible but adequate protection.

If the buyer's insurance will not cover the seller after the transaction, then there are a number of insurance alternatives available to sellers.

- *Self-Insurance.* This alternative is not prudent— no design professional should put his assets at risk for such claims.

- *Run-Off Policy.* This coverage is purchased by the seller from its insurer. The underwriters determine the availability and cost of such protection based on past history. Such a policy affords protection for claims made up to a fixed number of years after the effective transaction date, with an opportunity to review. A word of caution— the policy may not cover the applicable time period within which a claim may be made, in which case an uninsured exposure could exist. The amount of coverage and the size of the deductible is a function of the seller's risk analysis of a claim.

- *Retired Professionals Policy.* This type of insurance only covers individuals, and is not applicable to the entire firm. It is generally limited to principals of small firms which are liquidating, or to persons who wish to have more control of the risk when the buyer is willing to cover the seller's prior acts. Again, issues of cost, amount of coverage, and deductible will need to be resolved.

- *Extended Reporting Period.* This endorsement purchased by the seller from its insurer extends the time within which a claim, based on acts prior to the expiration date of the seller's last policy, may be made and reported. Since the extended period is often one year, this alternative may not make much sense for the seller.

Each of the alternatives discussed above are usually less desirable than having the buyer's insurance coverage absorb such risks. However, in cases where the buyer's coverage is not as broad, has lower limits and/or higher deductibles, the seller may very well wish to explore its own coverage for acts that precede the transaction.

Buyer's Issues

Buyers need to make sure there is a smooth transition in coverage, and there should be some concern for how the seller plans to insure prior acts. Since the seller's principals often become employees of the buyer, it is in everyone's interest that the seller be adequately protected.

- *Buyer's Purchase of Assets.* In an asset transaction, the buyer purchases only specific assets, and therefore assumes only the liabilities associated with those assets. The seller's policy would still cover prior acts, but the buyer

Professional Liability Information Alert

Figure 8-4

Issues such as cultural compatibility and effects on markets and services are commonly addressed early in merger or acquisition discussions. Insurance and liability issues are usually an afterthought, says Michael Heatwole, vice president of **Ames & Gough Insurance Agency, Inc.** (McLean, VA). "People always seem to bring liability up at the last second," says Heatwole, whose firm specializes in A/E professional liability. "It's usually the last thing they think about."

Ames & Gough periodically publishes an *Information Alert* for its clients. One issue contained the following recommendations for buyers:

We recommend that the buyer review the seller's 10-year claims history, and that said history include both an annual summary and an overall summary of the following information:

- *Insurer(s)*
- *Copies of all liability policies*
- *Policy period*
- *Policy limits*
- *Deductible*
- *Annual premium*
- *Closed claims, including any details involving a payment by the insurer*
- *Open claims, including details from the insurer and defense counsel regarding the relevant facts and an estimate of potential liability*
- *10-year paid and incurred loss ratios which will clearly demonstrate the relationship between premiums collected by an insurer and claims paid above the deductible. Unfavorable loss ratios should be fully explored by the buyer as potential evidence of poor management and/or inattention to professional standards on the part of the seller.*
- *Internal claim costs, including those incurred by the seller in time lost due to assisting in the defense effort, as well as those related to deductible obligations*

Reprinted with permission from Ames & Gough Insurance Agency, Inc.

Limiting a Buyer's Liability

Figure 8-5

It's the kind of horror story that causes A/E/P and environmental consulting firm principals to wake up at 3 a.m. in a sweat. An arbitrator told **Smith Technologies Corp.** (Newport Beach, CA) it owed a group of plaintiffs $4.5 million for its failure to adequately operate a battery component recycling and processing plant in Portland, Oregon. The award was apparently not covered by liability insurance, and the company said it couldn't pay without doing major damage to itself.

The contract that contained the arbitration clause used in the decision against Smith was originally drawn up with **Canonie Environmental Services, Inc.** (Dallas, TX), a firm Smith acquired in 1994. And while Smith's problems did not stem from Canonie's design of the plant, the ruling against Smith was related to Canonie's operation of the plant. The situation was an example of a buyer getting stuck with the liability for something the seller did prior to a merger or acquisition.

Experts say it's not unusual for a buyer to overlook certain liability issues in the heat of talks. But what can the leaders of a buying form do to reduce their chances of being held liable for something the selling firm did before the merger or acquisition took place? Here are a few suggestions:

1. Keep lawyers and insurance agents informed. Firm leaders too often rush deep into a deal before calling in the legal and insurance experts.

2. Be cautious if the selling firm provides non-traditional services or delivery methods. The buyer should be particularly wary if it does not provide the same non-traditional services or delivery methods as the seller. A firm could have most of its professional services liability covered, but the seller's non-traditional services might not be.

3. Consider a run-off or retired professionals policy. These usually leave the liability with the seller, with the issue of who pays for the policy to be worked out. The policy should ideally afford protection for claims made up to five years after the inception date of the policy, with the opportunity to renew for an additional five years. The retired professionals policy is usually for principals of small firms who are cashing out. Chris Poole, president of **Poole Professional, Ltd.** (Wakefield, MA), an insurance agency which specializes in coverage for design professionals, says his rule of thumb in pricing a run-off policy is to add up three years of the selling firm's premiums and divide by two. The retired professionals policy is usually for principals of small firms who are cashing out.

4. Roll all the liability into the buyer's policy. Some buyers balk at this because the seller is usually smaller and carries lower premiums and lower deductibles. It may be cheaper to negotiate the price and keep the liability with the seller.

would be responsible for the assets, contracts, and liabilities which it assumes. These should be noted in the buyer's policy.

- *Buyer's Purchase of Stock.* In a stock transaction, liability for the seller's prior acts are completely assumed by buyer. The transaction documents, however, can be drafted to require the seller (either through self-insurance or through coverage purchased by the seller), to indemnify the buyer for claims relating to the period prior to the transaction date.

If the transaction document is going to include an indemnity provision, the buyer must use the due diligence investigation to determine the financial strength behind the indemnity. If the individual owners of the seller are backing up the indemnity— or if a portion of the consideration paid to the seller is meant to back up the indemnity— the parties need to discuss whether an escrow is appropriate.

If the seller is purchasing coverage, the buyer should also explore the financial strength of the seller's insurer. The buyer may want to be insured under any policy purchased by the seller for the period prior to the effective date of the transaction. The buyer should also consider purchasing coverage in excess of the seller's coverage, to guarantee that policy limits are adequate.

Insurance Post-Transaction

The parties also need to discuss the coverage to be carried by the buyer after the transaction is completed. All services, including new services performed by the seller, will need to be covered. What is the proper amount of coverage for the combined entity? What would be a prudent deductible? Finally, in reviewing the cost of the transaction, buyers need to factor in premium increases due to expanded volume of services, in addition to limit and service increases.

Corporate Culture

Much of the literature describing mergers and acquisitions in professional service firms discusses the importance of the intangible known as "corporate culture." Corporate culture is difficult to describe and even more difficult to measure. The best way to begin to understand another company's corporate culture is to experience it— visit the offices, talk with the management, employees, and clients, and review the company's records, all of which can be easily accomplished as a part of the due diligence process.

One way to measure a firm's corporate culture is to have your management consultant do it under the auspices of conducting a management audit. This gives the consultant an opportunity to talk with employees about operations and management without making them worry about the firm being sold. The goal is to determine how similar are the two companies in terms of corporate culture. Before the transaction documents are signed, it is important for both the buyer and the seller to know if there will be any problems assimilating the two corporate cultures after the closing.

History and Ownership

Clues to a firm's stability can often be found in information about the firm's history and ownership. When was the firm founded, and how was past ownership transition implemented? Is there one dominant stockholder, a small dominant group, or is stock dispersed over a larger group?

Corporate Culture as a Deal Breaker

Figure 8-6

What issue is most likely to send principals considering a merger or acquisition running for the exit? For many principals in the A/E/P and environmental consulting business, noticeable differences in corporate culture can extinguish a deal before the flame is even lit.

"In my opinion, it's one of the most important factors, if not the most important," says Bill Mossbarger, president of **Fuller, Mossbarger, Scott & May, Inc.** (Lexington, KY), a 140-person geotechnical firm. "I'm talking about having the same philosophy about the type of engineering and quality of service. We pride ourselves in quality. We would hope the fit would be such that the employees we'd take on would feel the same way we do."

"Corporate culture is certainly one of the top three benefits we look for in any acquisition," says Lawrence Dooley, a former division president of **Day & Zimmermann International, Inc.** (Philadelphia, PA), a 12,000-person consulting engineering firm. "We look for a lot of different things, but a cultural fit is always in the top three. We look at the quality and values of key staff and how it matches with our values," he says. "We look for the opportunity where one plus one equals three— that's to say that the combination of the targeted company plus our company will be a greater value than the sum of the individual firms. That's what we look for."

Since the goal of most mergers or acquisitions is to create more value in each entity by combining them, a good fit is essential. Trying to force together cultures that don't mesh is an almost certain path to trouble. Finding a company that can effectively combine its capabilities with yours isn't easy, but it's sure to improve the likelihood of success for the new venture.

Leadership and Corporate Governance

How have changes in leadership evolved over the life of the firm? Does the current leadership team obtain its power because of its stock ownership or seniority? Or is the leadership team democratically elected? Does the company consult a cross section of the staff in making critical decisions, or are decisions made by a small group? Do younger firm members participate in the administrative aspects of the practice, such as dealing with attorneys, accountants, insurance professionals, banks? Are functional areas such as human resources, marketing, accounting properly staffed and running smoothly? Is the firm overly bureaucratic in operations? Are any systems lacking?

Staff Members

Have senior staff "grown up" in the firm or have people joined the firm laterally at senior positions? Are there clear career paths and a history of advancement within the firm? Is there unusually high turnover in the employee ranks?

Employee Benefits

Does the firm have competitive benefits for its employees? How do those benefits compare to those offered at your firm? Do the principals have uniform benefits or do senior staff have excessive and abusive benefits?

Quality of Services

Does the firm have a reputation for turning out high quality work? Do contracts and engagement letters reflect a reasoned, prudent approach to delivery services?

Organizational Chart

Does the formal organization chart reflect the actual operations? Are there people who are more important or less important to operations than the chart suggests?

Incentives

Is the firm mainly revenue driven or is quality of service important? How responsive is the firm to the needs of clients?

Acquiring a Family Business

Figure 8-7

Buying a family business is rarely an easy, painless process. And the situation can be even more difficult when the seller is family-owned. Someone looking into buying a family-owned A/E/P or environmental consulting firm has to ask: "Am I buying all of the family members as employees?"

The question is rhetorical. The buyer's answer is, "I can't." In most cases, you're going to find that there are family members in positions only because they are family members.

Buyers must approach the issue of dead-weight family members tactfully, but aggressively. It's important to address the situation so problems don't crop up late in the acquisition process, but buyers also shouldn't feel the need to bring the issue to a head immediately.

If it becomes clear that the buyer is going to have to accommodate a family member who might otherwise not warrant a position in the company, the buyer must make it clear to the seller that there is a cost. Whether it's a buy-out of that family member, moving that person to another position in the firm, or some other special arrangement, the buyer will expect to be compensated in some way for making special accommodations.

Another way to handle this situation is to make it clear that you're not guaranteeing employment agreements to all family members. When the time is up, if a family member hasn't proven him- or herself, the buyer can point to the door. You don't have to say right up front that a certain person doesn't figure into long-range plans, but you've got to make it clear that a family member will only be able to work for the company if they earn the right to—they're not related to the person who founded the company anymore.

Three Important Due Diligence Considerations Figure 8-8

The most important fact-finding in a due diligence investigation, principals say, is done not by lawyers but by the managers from the buying firm. Here are three items for special attention:

Staff: The heart of any acquisition. You must understand the capabilities and goals of all the key people in the organization prior to making an offer. If the seller pleads his desire for secrecy, watch out. In one case, an engineering firm seller wanted to negotiate a deal without informing anyone else in the company, including his *son*, a key manager. Negotiations dissolved over the issue.

Continuing contracts: The percentage of completion versus the amount billed on contracts can be a deal breaker. One prospective buyer learned of a $1 million project at the last minute that needed to be completely re-done— they only found out about it by interviewing a project manager at the selling firm. In deals where only *assets* are purchased, most contracts (including standard AIA and ACEC agreements) are not *assignable*— i.e., you can't have someone else complete them without the client's permission. Fortunately, clients don't usually want to switch horses in mid-stream. But they've been known to pull projects that were awarded but not yet begun.

Different methods of accounting: The contract problem is compounded by the diverse methods of accounting in our industry. We've seen everything. One firm classified all time as billable. Another included proposals in backlog. And in the case of sole proprietorships, separating the firm's finances from the owner's finances can be difficult.

"You have to know all the information about the firm you're acquiring," says Tom Veratti, founder of **CON-TEST, Inc.** (East Longmeadow, MA), a 180-person environmental firm. "You have to be very thorough during due diligence. Make sure there are no surprises."

These questions will give each party an understanding of the philosophy, practices, and evolution of the other firm. Throughout the due diligence investigation, keep these issues in mind when collecting data and you will be well prepared for the integration and transition which follow the closing.

Results of Due Diligence

The completion of the due diligence process marks a significant milestone in the transaction process. If conducted properly, the due diligence investigation will yield valuable information in three areas:

First, the investigation serves to confirm information about the other firm. You will have information on things that you either knew superficially or assumed to be the case. This information forms the basis for the representations and warranties contained in the transition documents and their corresponding schedules.

The investigation also identifies issues that need to be evaluated prior to the closing. Information obtained in the due diligence experience which is inconsistent with previous information, or which is unexpected and troublesome, forms an agenda of issues to be addressed, negotiated and resolved in the process of drafting and finalizing the transition documents.

Lastly, the due diligence process allows the parties to gather information which will be useful in the post-closing integration of the firms. Planning for things like discrepancies in employee benefits before the firms are actually combined can help make the transition more successful.

Conclusion

Collecting information as part of the due diligence investigation gives both parties a chance to investigate the details of each other's operations. Both parties have the responsibility of conducting an investigation thorough enough to identify any issues which might stand in the way of a transaction.

The previous efforts in analyzing the tax and corporate aspects of the transaction (Chapter 6), negotiating and executing a letter of intent (Chapter 7), and gathering and distilling the results of the due diligence investigation all come together in the preparation and negotiation of the transaction documents, which are covered in Chapter 9.

9 The Transaction Documents

- Introduction
- The Purchase & Sale Agreement
- Representations, Warranties, Covenants, and Agreements
  - Representations and Warranties of the Seller
  - Representations and Warranties of the Stockholders
  - Representations and Warranties of the Buyer
  - Covenants and Agreements
- Purposed Served By the Representations and Warranties
  - Disclosure and Assessment of the Seller
  - Conditions to Closing and Allocation of Risk
- Indemnification
  - Risk Identification and Allocation Alternatives
- Schedules to the Purchase & Sale Agreement
- Exhibits to the Purchase & Sale Agreement
- Employment, Consulting, and Non-Competition Agreements
- Buyer's Financing Documents
- Buyer's Stockholders' Agreement
- Conclusion

Chapter 9

The Transaction Documents

☑ *The transaction documents, led by the Purchase & Sale Agreement (P&S), represent the final, written expression of the business deal.*

Introduction

In Chapter 6, the analysis of the tax and corporate issues related to the transaction refined the specifics of the deal from the viewpoint of both the seller and the buyer. In Chapter 7, we explained the role of the letter of intent which sets forth the outline of the proposed transaction, subject to various contingencies including due diligence. And in Chapter 8, the due diligence exercise confirmed the salient facts relating to the buyer and seller and identified specific issues and problems to be addressed.

The result of all three of these tasks comes together in the transaction documents, which supersede all previous written and oral understandings. These documents become the defining agreements between and among the parties, and will serve to define the rights of parties regarding any issues or problems that may arise after the closing. The definitive transaction documentation to buy, sell or merge is generally comprised of the following:

- the Purchase & Sale Agreement (P&S);
- schedules and exhibits to the P&S;
- employment, consulting, and/or non-competition agreements;
- the buyer's financing documents; and
- the buyer's stockholders' agreement.

The Purchase & Sale Agreement

The Purchase & Sale Agreement (P&S) outlines and sets forth the basic business deal, including a comprehensive description of the seller. Depending on the nature of the transaction, the P&S may also include a description of the buyer. A sample P&S outline is included as Appendix E.

It is common that the drafting and negotiation of the P&S will begin while the due diligence is being completed and the schedules are being finalized. The P&S is drawn up by the buyer's attorney.

Representations, Warranties, Covenants, and Agreements

The substance of the seller's concern and the primary focus of the P&S is the representations, warranties, covenants, and agreements of the seller and some or all of its stockholders. The sections on representations and warranties generally outline the substance of what it is that the seller has to sell, as well as exactly what the buyer thinks is being purchased. The section on covenants and agreements gives an outline of what the parties agree will happen after the deal.

These attachments are usually divided into different sections, including Representations and Warranties of the Seller, Representations and Warranties of the Stockholders, Representations and Warranties of the Buyer, and Covenants and Agreements.

Representations and Warranties of the Seller

The section covering the representations and warranties of the seller usually includes the following:

- Organization and Qualification
- Authority to Execute and Perform Agreements
- Capitalization and Title to Shares
- Subsidiaries and Other Affiliates
- Articles of Organization; By-Laws
- Financial Statements
- Absence of Undisclosed Liabilities
- No Material Adverse Change
- Tax Matters
- Compliance with Laws
- No Breach
- Actions and Proceedings
- Contracts and Other Agreements
- Bank Accounts and Powers of Attorney
- Properties (Real or Personal)
- Intellectual Property
- Clients
- Liens
- Accounts Receivable
- Employee Benefit Plans

- Employee Relations
- Environmental Matters
- Transactions with Management
- Insurance
- Brokerage
- Hazardous Material

Representations and Warranties of the Stockholders

The section describing the representations and warranties of the stockholders usually includes the following:

- Authority to Execute and Perform Agreements
- No Breach
- Title to Shares
- Investment Intent
- Accuracy of Seller Representations and Warranties

Representations and Warranties of the Buyer

The sections that are typically included as representations and warranties of the buyer are the following:

- Organization
- Authority to Execute and Perform Agreement
- Capitalization
- Financial Statements
- Absence of Undisclosed Liabilities
- No Material Adverse Change
- Tax Matters
- Compliance with Laws
- Actions and Proceedings
- Employee Benefit Plans
- No Breach

- Hazardous Materials
- Clients
- Brokerage
- Disclosure

Covenants and Agreements

The following points are usually covered in the section on covenants and agreements:

- Seller's Employees
- Accrued Sick Pay
- Insurance Coverage Continuation
- Noncompetition, Non-Solicitation and Confidentiality
- Expenses
- Further Assurances

Purpose Served By the Representations, Warranties, Covenants, and Agreements

The representations, warranties, covenants, and agreements of the seller contained in the P&S (whether a stock purchase agreement or an asset purchase agreement) and the accompanying schedules describing specific issues relating to the seller, serve several different purposes at different times in the acquisition process, including disclosure and assessment of the seller, identification of the conditions to closing and allocation of risk, and provision for indemnification.

Disclosure and Assessment of the Seller

Prior to the closing, the representations, warranties, covenants, agreements, and schedules provide information about the seller and its affairs which enables the buyer to identify and quantify the risks associated with the acquisition and confirm the buyer's assessment of the seller.

Conditions to Closing and Allocation of Risk

Prior to the closing, representations, warranties and covenants also serve as a benchmark for the buyer's right to elect not to consummate a transaction or to consummate the transaction on different terms by allocating some or all of the risks associated with the problems disclosed in the representations and warranties to the seller or the seller's stockholders.

Indemnification

Following the closing, to the extent that any representation, warranty, covenant or scheduled information is determined to have been untrue or incomplete, the representations, warranties, and covenants provide the buyer with a basis upon which to seek compensation for losses incurred due to such untrue, incomplete or omitted information.

Risk Identification and Allocation Alternatives

Particular problem areas of the seller and its business are identified either prior to execution of the acquisition agreement through disclosure in the representations, warranties and schedules, or after execution of the acquisition agreement but prior to the closing, through updated representations, warranties and schedules and review of the seller's compliance with covenants during such period.

These problems must be categorized according to their respective levels of risk and the buyer must determine which if any of these risks it will assume and how the risks it will not assume will be addressed. There are a number of different kinds of risks as they apply the agreement. The following paragraphs provide a brief sketch of the different problem areas, but you should consult your attorney in order to determine how each of these risks applies to your particular transaction.

Risks in the Ordinary Course Which are Not Material to the Acquisition

No business is perfect and therefore in any transaction the buyer will be faced with claims or issues which arise in the ordinary course of running a business and, although they need to be addressed and resolved, are not material to the business and should not cause the buyer to seek compensation from the seller or its stockholders.

Material Risks Which Can be Quantified and Resolved by Payment of Money

To the extent a problem is identified which is material to the acquisition and is readily quantifiable, the buyer has several alternatives. The buyer may:

- proceed with the transaction, reduce the purchase price, and assume responsibility for the problem;
- withhold or defer a portion of the purchase price and only pay it upon, or set off against it in connection with, resolution of the problem;
- proceed with the transaction on the condition that the seller or the seller's stockholders agree to retain responsibility for the problem, directly or through indemnification with an escrow fund; or
- decide not to go forward with the transaction at all.

Material Risks Which Cannot be Readily Quantified

To the extent a material or potentially material problem is identified but cannot be quantified, either because insufficient facts exist at the time of the transaction or because the risk is dependent upon the actions of third parties which have not yet occurred, the buyer has all of the alternatives set forth above. However, obviously, under these circumstances the buyer may be less willing to proceed with the transaction because the financial resources necessary to remedy the problem cannot be quantified and therefore a purchase price reduction, escrow or holdback, regardless of amount, may not necessarily be sufficient to compensate the buyer for assuming the risk.

Indemnification also may not necessarily be sufficient to compensate the buyer for assuming the risk. Furthermore, indemnification may not be a viable solution if it is unclear whether the seller or the seller's stockholders will have and will retain sufficient financial resources following the transaction to satisfy the liability. The buyer may decide to abandon the transaction under these circumstances.

Risks Based on the Receipt of Third Party Consents and Approvals to the Transaction

To the extent the buyer identifies that a certain contract, employee, governmental permit, license or other arrangement is necessary or material to the seller's business, the buyer will condition consummation of the transaction upon receipt of such consents, licenses or permits or the execution of an assignment on or prior to the closing. Under certain circumstances the buyer may waive such a condition and consummate the transaction with the seller, but only after a determination that the receipt of the particular consent or approval which will not occur prior to the closing, is highly likely to be forthcoming after the closing, and an agreement by the seller or the seller's stockholders to escrow a portion of the purchase price to protect the buyer in the event the consent or approval is not obtained.

Indemnification

As noted above, there are various methods of allocating risk between the seller (and the seller's stockholders) and the buyer, such as the retention by the seller or the seller's stockholders of certain liabilities, the buyer's deferral of the payment (with a promissory note) of a portion of the purchase price with a right of set off by the buyer in the event the risk is realized, escrow of a portion of the purchase price to provide ready assets to fund the problem, the buyer's payment of a portion of the purchase price on a contingent basis only upon the occurrence or the nonoccurrence of certain future events (such as an earnout), seller and seller's stockholder's indemnification of the buyer, or a combination of one or more of the foregoing.

The indemnification provisions in an acquisition agreement generally provide for the seller (either the seller, the seller's stockholders, or both) to indemnify the buyer for losses (including professional fees and costs of defense of any claims) arising out of misrepresentations or omissions of material facts in the seller's representations and warranties, or a breach of any of the seller's covenants contained in the acquisition agreement. Indemnification may also be required, depending on the particular transaction, for specific matters disclosed in the representations, warranties, covenants involving risks for which the buyer does not want responsibility, but which do not cause the buyer to walk away entirely from the transaction.

The following is a summary of some of the common methods by which a seller's indemnification obligations to the buyer can be limited, and thereby reallocate risk in the transaction.

Baskets

Generally a seller will negotiate for a basket, which is an amount of losses which must be incurred by the buyer before the buyer can make a claim for indemnification. The size of the basket is a subject for negotiation and obviously, the buyer likes small or nonexistent baskets and the seller favors large baskets. The average basket is often in the range of 1% to 2% of the purchase price. In the event the basket amount is reached, another issue which may arise is whether or not the buyer has the right to collect all losses from indemnification claims from the first claim dollar or whether the buyer bears the loss up to the amount of the basket and the seller's indemnification obligation is only for the amount of claims which exceed the basket. Obviously, the latter approach is more favorable to the seller, but this point should be clearly addressed in the transaction documentation.

A basket can also be limited to certain types of claims or only claims in excess of certain dollar amounts, so as to create different baskets for different risks. Lastly, to the extent the representations and warranties in the acquisition agreement contain qualifications which permit disclosure in certain instances of only information which is material to the seller's business or are limited to information about which seller's stockholders or certain officers of the seller have actual knowledge, the seller's indemnification obligations to the buyer are further diluted.

Caps on the Seller's Indemnification

Often a seller will seek to have a buyer agree to a "cap" or a ceiling on the seller's indemnification obligation, so that regardless of the actual loss arising out of a breach of a representation, warranty or covenant by a seller, or other seller-indemnifiable claim, in no event will the seller be obligated to indemnify the buyer in excess of a dollar amount. Again the cap can apply to all claims or can be limited to only certain categories of claims and is wholly the result of negotiation by the parties.

In transactions involving the sale of stock, where there may be passive or small minority investors who have had no involvement with the target company's management, the buyer may be willing to cap such stockholder's indemnification obligations to the buyer at an amount equal to the proceeds received by such stockholders as a result of the transaction.

Survival Period for Indemnification Claims

Generally, the acquisition agreement will designate the period of time following the closing during which the buyer can make claims against the seller for indemnification. A survival period of 12 to 24 months is typical for most of the issues addressed in the representations and warranties. Often the survival period will be extended to a longer period of time for matters relating to taxes, environmental liabilities, and ERISA liabilities. The extended periods for these liabilities will often be for the duration of the statute of limitation for taxes and as long as 6 to 10 years, or longer, for the other matters depending on the particular circumstances.

Again the survival period is a subject for negotiation by the parties. The buyer requires a sufficiently long survival period to discover problems, often one financial audit period at least, whereas the seller obviously wants to put the transaction behind it and known that after a certain date, claims for indemnification can no longer be made under the acquisition agreement.

Tax and Insurance Effects

The seller will also often want the acquisition agreement to provide that any indemnifiable losses for which the seller is responsible shall be reduced by any tax benefits or insurance proceeds received by the buyer in connection with the claim, so the buyer is not compensated for an indemnifiable claim in excess of its actual loss.

Individual or Joint Liability

Often in the case of a sale of stock involving multiple stockholders, the buyer will want the seller's stockholders to be jointly responsible for any indemnification claims so it does not have to proceed against each and every stockholder to collect on a claim. Obviously, each of the selling stockholders will want to only be responsible for their portion of the claim and not the entire claim— they do not want to be the guarantors of their fellow sellers. Sometimes, where there are different categories of stockholders, such as large stockholders who have been actively involved in the business and passive investors or small minority stockholders, the buyer will agree to individual and not joint liability for the small minority or passive investors and will limit their liability to certain kinds of claims, such as breaches of their representations as to good title and authority to sell. To the extent the buyer insists on joint liability, the stockholders will want to enter into an agreement, providing for contribution apportioning any liability among themselves.

Exclusivity

The seller will always want a provision in the acquisition agreement which provides that indemnification is the sole and exclusive remedy for breaches of the acquisition agreement so that it can be assured that a breach of contract or other claim will not be brought by the buyer which could increase the seller's damages to the buyer by avoiding any basket, cap or other limiting provisions contained in the acquisition agreement.

Collateral for Indemnification

The seller should also keep in mind that any escrow, deferred purchase price payment (like a promissory note), holdback, or contingent purchase price (like an earnout) serves as an available funding resource from which the buyer will seek compensation for any losses, either directly or to back up indemnification obligations. The terms, including the amounts, timing, and procedures of all of such arrangements, should be carefully reviewed and are the subject of much negotiation by the parties.

Schedules to the Purchase & Sale Agreement

The representations, warranties and covenants set forth in the P&S are critically important to defining the liabilities of the seller after the transaction closing. The schedules contain the information which serves as the basis for these representations and warranties. Therefore, the schedules should be complete and provide full explanations— be sure that nothing gets left out. It is also important for all exceptions to be clearly delineated so there are no inadvertent misstatements.

Outline for an Employment, Consulting, or Non-Competition Agreement

Figure 9-1

Articulated either as part of the letter of intent or in the final transaction documents, employment, consulting, or non-compete agreements may apply to particular employees or affiliated companies.

1. Parties
2. Engagement and Term
3. Position and Duties
4. Compensation
5. Termination
    - a. Cause
    - b. Not for Cause
    - c. Disability
    - d. Death
6. Covenant Not to Compete
    - a. Time Frame
    - b. Geographical Territory
    - c. Type of Activity
7. Non-Solicitation of Clients/Employees
8. Trade Secrets
9. Confidential Information
10. Injunctive Relief
11. Arbitration
12. Miscellaneous
    - a. Binding Effect
    - b. Entire Agreement
    - c. Counterparts & Governing Law
13. Notices

Exhibits to the Purchase & Sale Agreement

The purpose of appending certain operative documents (i.e., sample closing documents) as exhibits to the P&S is to have the parties agree on their content and structure prior to the actual closing. This is done in an attempt to prevent issues or surprises from arising when the parties are all gathered to sign the final transaction documents.

Employment, Consulting, and Non-Competition Agreements

As we mentioned in Chapter 7, these agreements often are a part of the deal, and were previously included in the letter of intent. They should, however, be included in the final transaction documentation. An outline of these types of agreements can be found in Figure 9-1.

From the point of view of the seller's stockholders— who are restricted by the provisions— the most important aspects of these agreements are as follows:

- With what corporate entity is the agreement being made? If the seller will be operated as a separate subsidiary of the buyer, the executive should try to have the buyer, as the parent of the seller, guarantee the agreement.

- What is the exact job description? To whom will the employee report?

- Carefully read and understand the scope and breadth of the covenants not to compete and not to solicit clients and/or employees. How long do they continue?

- Under what circumstances can the employee be terminated? Is there a severance payment if the employee dies, becomes disabled, or is involuntarily terminated?

Buyer's Financing Documents

If the buyer is financing the transaction, it will be signing a promissory note, loan agreement, or a security agreement which encumbers the assets of the seller. The buyer may also sign a pledge agreement, securing the newly acquired equity stock of the seller.

While these documents are the primary concern of the buyer, the seller should be aware of several issues:

- If part of the cash purchase price is being deferred, do the financing documents and the debt secured thereby either restrict or add risk to the likelihood that payment will be made to the seller?

- If part of the purchase consideration is stock in the buyer, does the debt being taken on by the buyer diminish the value of the stock? Do the financing documents prohibit the redemption of stock?

Buyer's Stockholders' Agreement

Appendix F outlines a form of stockholders' agreement. If some of the transaction consideration is being paid in stock of the buyer, then the terms of the buyer's stockholders' agreement is of importance to the principals of the seller. After all, the exit strategy to liquidate the purchase price is subject to the terms of this agreement. The seller's ultimate exit strategy must be to liquidate the stock at some point now or in the future. Any sale of stock will be subject to the buyer's stockholders' agreement.

The most important items to focus on are the following:

- What is the formula for determining the purchase price?

- Based on age, how many of the principals of the buyer are likely to retire before the principals of the seller? If there is a significant number of stockholders who likely will retire, can the buyer support the payments? Where will those payments come from - cash flow, new stockholder purchases, financing?

- Is there insurance to fund the buyout in the case of death or disability of a principal?

- If the payout is to be made over time, as is commonplace, is there security for the payout? What is the recourse for non-payout?

Conclusion

At this point, the transactions documents have been negotiated, drafted, reviewed, and agreed on, and they replace all previous agreements and understandings. They are the definitive transaction documents, and to the extent that they are complete, they will resolve any disagreements that may arise between the parties after the closing.

Once the transaction documents have been finalized, the parties are ready to make other necessary closing preparations. Chapter 10 discusses these additional preparations, the actual closing, and the integration process that follows the closing. In addition, Chapter 10 will help you to understand how to measure the success of your transaction.

10 The Closing and Integration

- Introduction
- Preparation for Closing
- Operational Tasks Relating to the Closing
    - Payroll Processing
    - Employee Benefits
    - Retirement Plans
    - Insurance Coverage
    - Accounting/Financial Matters
    - Publicity
- Post-Closing Business Plan
- The Closing
- Integration
    - Material Integration
    - Systems Integration
    - Cultural Integration
- Changing the Name of the Company
- What is a Successful Transaction?
- Conclusion

Chapter 10

The Closing and Integration

☑ *As the closing approaches, the transaction partners primarily focus on preparing for the closing and on the issues related to the integration of the two firms.*

Introduction

Once the deal documentation has been finalized, the parties and their advisors turn to the preparation and completion of the closing. This includes the following three steps:

- performing tasks to consummate the transaction;
- performing operational tasks relating to the immediate post-closing period; and
- preparing the post-closing strategic business plan.

Preparation for Closing

This portion of the project is driven primarily by the lawyers. Figure 10-1 provides a checklist of the tasks that will need to be completed. The preparation, revisions and implementation of the checklist is nothing more than "in the trenches" work which must be attacked one step at a time.

Depending upon the form of the transaction and the states of incorporation of the parties, the stockholders of the seller must vote at a meeting (asset sale) or they must each execute assignments of their respective stock (stock sale). Each stockholder, especially if there are stockholders who own small amounts of stock and who have not been involved in the transaction, must be given adequate time to review and assimilate all information. In either case, communications to stockholders must be well-written and clear.

Stockholders normally have several questions and concerns about the transactions, both with respect to the deal itself and regarding other deal issues such as continued employment, management of the seller, etc. It is strongly recommended that an informational meeting be held for the stockholders after the written materials have been distributed and prior to the formal vesting. This allows the stockholders to ask questions or confirm their understanding of the transaction.

If the buyer is financing the transaction, then completing the arrangements for financing is critical, in addition to addressing any remaining issues for the buyer or seller.

The usual tasks which govern the timing of the consummation of the transaction are the obtaining of third party consents such as contract assignments and lease assignments. It is here that the ongoing clients of the seller must be visited and their questions and concerns addressed to ensure that they consent to the assign-

Closing Preparation Checklist

Figure 10-1

Although your attorney will be driving the transaction at this point, you can use this checklist to guide you through the tasks that will need to be completed before the closing.

- ☐ Closing Memorandum and Checklist
- ☐ Definitive Purchase and Sale Agreement
- ☐ Schedules to Agreement
    - ☐ Remuneration
    - ☐ Contracts
    - ☐ Insurance in Force
    - ☐ Litigation
    - ☐ Title Exceptions
    - ☐ Trademarks
    - ☐ Certain Warranties
    - ☐ Insider Transactions
    - ☐ Pre-Closing Transactions

- ☐ Definitive Employment Agreements
- ☐ Escrow Agreement
- ☐ Powers of Attorney and Stock Escrow Agreements
- ☐ Certified Certificates of Incorporation
- ☐ By-Laws Certified by Secretaries
- ☐ Good-Standing Certificates
- ☐ Tax Status and Lien Docket Certificates
- ☐ Certified Resolutions
- ☐ Representation Certificates
- ☐ Consents
- ☐ Assignments, if applicable
- ☐ Resignations of Certain Directors and Officers, if applicable
- ☐ Assignments of Patents, Trademarks, and Copyrights
- ☐ Assignment of Bank Accounts
- ☐ Legal Opinions
- ☐ Checks
- ☐ Promissory Notes
- ☐ Cross-Receipt

ment of contracts. A client will want to know whether the team working on its project will remain intact and whether the services will remain at the same (or improved) level as before the transaction.

Employees are a crucial topic in the pre-closing period. Emotional issues including denial, fear, acceptance and even enthusiasm may be present. Thus, the employees must be addressed and their questions answered. Be honest, as people's careers are at stake. It is good practice for the buyer to have its senior people meet with seller's employees to discuss the vision of the transaction and why each employee should be enthused to be joining the buyer.

Operational Tasks Relating to the Closing

There are a number of operational tasks that must be completed prior to the closing which ensure a smooth and orderly transition as of the effective closing date of the closing.

Payroll Processing

If the buyer is changing the processing of the payroll of the employees of the seller, then appropriate arrangements for such transition must be made.

Employee Benefits

Employee benefits such as group life and disability insurance, group health and dental insurance, vacation and sick days, etc. are a high priority to employees. Therefore, if any one or more of these plans will be affected by the transaction, it is important that changeovers be performed without disrupting employee coverage. It is especially important to compare the benefits offered by both firms to determine if any employees will experience a serious reduction in benefits as a result of the transaction— increasing employee benefits is easy, but taking them away can be harder. And the people aspect of employee benefits is often worthy of more consideration than the logistics of combining everyone under one policy.

Retirement Plans

The treatment of the seller's retirement plans deserves appropriate attention. If the seller's plans are being terminated and the employees of seller becoming participants in the buyer's plan, then the effective date of the closing serves as the cross-over date for such change.

Insurance Coverage

All the insurance coverage for the seller's operations, including professional liability insurance, must switch over as of the closing date.

Accounting and Financial Matters

If the buyer is switching the accounting and financial operations of seller to the centralized function of buyer, then these arrangements must be in place as of the effective date of the transactions.

War Story: Bringing Computer Systems Together

Figure 10-2

THE INTEGRATION of computer systems is one area that does not always receive the attention it deserves. Here's the story of how one firm addressed the issue of technological compatibility following an acquisition.

EARTH TECH (Long Beach, CA), a 1,900-employee environmental consulting firm, has been an active acquirer of small and mid-sized engineering and environmental consulting firms. Due to its buying spree, the firm's 40 offices were using seven different systems for project management, accounting, and financial reporting.

In December 1995, EARTH TECH was on the other end of the M&A equation. The firm was acquired by **Tyco International** (Exeter, NH), a nearly $5 billion manufacturing company. The transaction spurred EARTH TECH to examine its own computer systems, which led to the decision to consolidate with Tyco into one system. The aggressive goal was to have the system up and running in July, the beginning of the firm's fiscal year.

The entire process, from the initial go-ahead to the system going live, took only one year. King Nelson, the former director of information systems for EARTH TECH, explains how the company was able to achieve its goal. "To start, we looked at what resources we need," says Nelson. "We spent a lot of time to find the best project accounting package for us. We wanted a database that we could use for other things."

After an extensive search, the firm settled on Oracle Financials. This package was chosen at least partly due to its emphasis on project accounting. "Because we are an engineering firm, project accounting drives everything. With many other packages, project accounting is not a major module," says Nelson.

Once the package was selected, EARTH TECH had to undertake the massive task of coordinating 40 offices using seven different systems. It started by assigning a full-time project manager, Paul Grice, and assembling a dedicated team for the project.

One of the first decisions the team made was to combine all the different systems into the new system at the same time. This effort was facilitated by having at least one person in each office work with the team. One of the most daunting tasks was the actual data conversion. Nelson estimated that EARTH TECH currently has between 12,000 and 15,000 open projects, all of which had to be converted into the new system. In addition to EARTH TECH's team, the firm brought in consultants from Oracle to assist with the data conversion. "Oracle helped us create the reports and modify the systems. They did a lot of work with us on data conversion," said Nelson.

Nelson did offer some words of wisdom for any firm that is converting or consolidating a computer system. "Get a good project team together. You need to have a project leader that can cajole, push, and prod," he says.

He also emphasizes the importance of planning and follow-through. "Pick a reasonable timeline and stick to it," he says. "We had plenty of chances to make excuses and stop in the middle. But we bit the bullet and finished the project."

Publicity

The announcement of the closing of the transaction, both internally to employees and externally to the profession, clients and competition should be well crafted.

Post-Closing Business Plan

The buyer, working with seller's management, must have formulated a business plan for the post-closing transition. Included in this business plan are marketing and cross-marketing of seller's services, operational issues such as the organization chart and personnel reassignments and terminations.

The Closing

The closing itself is an anticlimactic event. The effective date of the closing is often determined by convenience, such as the end of a week to allow for the billing of time to projects of the seller to correspond to a natural breakpoint. Using Monday as the effective date also allows for the parties to use the weekend to implement the transition of operational tasks.

The actual closing usually consists of the attorneys exchanging pre-signed documents with little, if any, activity among the principals. Often, the principals use the closing as a symbolic event to get together to congratulate each other, talk about the future, and begin with good feelings. A closing dinner or party can be used to kickoff the integration on a positive note.

Integration

The period following the closing involves the integration and assimilation of the transaction parties.

Often, the transaction documents contemplate post-closing adjustments in the purchase price. In addition, certain non-material consents which were not received prior to closing must be obtained. The closing documentation also governs any disputes or claims for issues with respect to representations and warranties. If the deal was an asset transaction, then the receivables of the seller must be collected and its liabilities paid. Thereafter, the seller will liquidate and dissolve its corporate form.

Integration of the three firms can be broken down into three general areas: material, systems, and cultural integration.

Material Integration

Material integration includes changing facilities or relocating employees if necessary. Other assets, like company vehicles, computer equipment, and software, should also be re-distributed, or made compatible. In addition, the firm may want to get rid of any resources that are not needed once the two entities have been combined.

Systems Integration

The integration of computer, accounting, and other systems is often the most difficult part of the transaction process. The key to integrating systems is to plan how the changes will be made, and to make the changeover soon as possible. This will minimize the disruption of operations, and quickly bring the company to the point of operating efficiently.

Integrating an Acquisition

Figure 10-3

Design and environmental consulting firms that have found an acquisition target and negotiated a deal *still* face what many principals believe is the most difficult part of the process— smoothly integrating the new firm into the old. "It's a long, tedious process that takes a tremendous amount of effort," says Tim Lowe, president of **Rosser Lowe Engineers** (Atlanta, GA), a 175-person A/E firm. "More than you can ever imagine until you've done it. But without integration, an acquisition will be a failure."

That's why most principals experienced in acquisitions stress finding a firm with a similar corporate culture— or at least one that is compatible in most ways. The more similarities you find in the acquired firm, the less painful the integration will be. "Four of our five acquisitions worked out well, but one wasn't a cultural fit," says Tom Veratti, founder of **CON-TEST, Inc.** (East Longmeadow, MA), a 180-person environmental firm. "The people there had been very much controlled by a small business owner. When they were put into our company, they just couldn't handle the freedom. They didn't know how to take responsibility themselves."

No matter how similar the firms are, however, you can expect some growing-together pains. "The thing that I think gets many acquisitions off on the wrong foot is the acquiring party begins by saying they're not going to change anything," says Frank Callahan, the former chairman/CEO at **Greiner Engineering, Inc.** (Irving, TX), a 1,500-person consulting engineering firm. "They'll say, 'You guys are doing a great job. We want you to continue the way you are.' If that were true, there would be no reason to do an acquisition."

Rich Hangen, president of **Vanasse Hangen Brustlin, Inc.** (Watertown, MA), a 350-person consulting engineering firm, says his company worked hard to make their two acquisitions feel welcome. "I think it was real important that in both cases, as soon as the ink was dry, I went down there and made presentations on what we're all about," says Hangen. "I wanted them to know I didn't have two heads."

Problems with integration don't only revolve around attitude and personal outlook. The acquiring firm also has to answer some important business aspects, like who will manage the acquired firm, whether employment contracts and/or non-compete agreements needed, and how discrepancies in salaries and benefits should be handled.

When an acquired firm isn't completely absorbed into the parent organization, the buying principals often prefer to send someone from their own management team to help ease the integration. "In every case that we didn't send a manager down, we've had problems," says Lawrence E. Newhart, a veteran of seven acquisitions and former president at **Day & Zimmermann, Inc.** (Philadelphia, PA), a 12,000-person A/E firm. "It's not that we don't trust people. It's that people have no sense of where the fence posts are unless you lead them through it."

Callahan says he tries to design his deals so both sides will benefit if the acquisition is a success. "If the after-acquisition performance of the acquired unit exceeds expectations, there should be a reward," he says. "If not, there should be a penalty."

Callahan says. "I don't think there's any way to *win* a negotiation," he says. "It needs to be a win-win. You have to have continuing goodwill from both sides for it to be a successful acquisition."

Cultural Integration

All parties must continue the work of the merger integration team to ensure that communication is fostered and open information shared. This post-closing oversight is important. Each party must respect the employees of the other party in daily working. Personnel changes, including termination, reassignments and restructuring the organization should be done and completed as soon after the change as possible. Networking between offices should be stressed. On site presence of the buyer's personnel with seller's former employees is often beneficial in integrating offices. Project teams should also be integrated to foster assimilation.

Changing the Name of the Company

Technically speaking, deciding on a name for a newly acquired firm is probably the easiest part of the whole process. But strategically and emotionally, it's a much larger issue. On one hand, it makes sense for acquiring firms to want their offices or divisions to have a common identity. On the other hand, allowing the acquired firm to retain its old name reassures clients and cashes in on the firm's goodwill.

Buyers really have only four options: to leave the acquired firm's name the same, to give the acquired firm a hybrid name, to give it a new name altogether, or to give the new firm the buyer's name. So how do you decide? Here are a number of things to consider:

The more established the firm is, the better to leave it's name alone. Tremendous confusion can be created if clients and employees don't stop referring to the firm by it's old name, and it is tough for acquired firms to "re-build" an old image in the marketplace.

Hybrid names sometimes let you have it both ways. You can retain the goodwill, and at the same time, use common marketing when it is needed. On the other hand, giving the firm an altogether new name can give you the worst of both worlds, and is very uncommon. A completely new name does not capitalize on the existing reputation of either firm, and will require a sizable marketing investment to make the industry aware of the new entity.

In most cases, the name of the acquired operation should be immediately changed to the parent's name. This doesn't mean that all of the acquired firm's goodwill is lost. A name change, handled properly, can be viewed as a positive by both employees and clients alike. It can also go a long way toward breaking down any "us-versus-them" feelings that crop up after the marriage. One name sends the clear message that you are one company.

Especially in the short term, changing names may involve a trade-off— the loss of an old name may hurt the firm in some ways, but could also help the firm in others. Be patient, plan for the long-term benefit when deciding on a name change, and once the change takes place, expect it to take some time for changes to sink in.

What is a Successful Transaction?

If you listen to the "experts," you could easily be convinced that it's darn near impossible to successfully acquire a firm. But "successful" does not just refer to getting the deal done. Instead, it extends to include integration, and is measured in part by how well the two firms become one.

Traits of a Successful Acquisition Figure 10-4

When it comes to successfully completing a deal in the A/E/P and environmental consulting industries, vision, knowledge, and process are the keys to success. Firms with the greater chance of success in a merger or acquisition have the following traits:

The principals have a clear understanding of the rationale for the transaction. The firm's principals need to determine if their goal is to add complementary services that will generate synergies with their existing in-house capabilities, to enter a new market through the acquisition of a particular client-base, or to establish a new geographic presence. If it is for reasons of geographic expansion, is the acquisition or merger designed to help the firm better serve the far-flung needs of existing clients, or to seize the opportunity of a "hot" region? Not only will these principals *know* the answers to these questions, they will explain the logic behind the proposed merger or acquisition in the company's strategic plan.

The principals have a good idea of the firm they want to buy or merge with. This *does not* necessarily mean they have a specific firm in mind. It *does* mean they have a defined set of criteria (such as market sector, geographic location, size, services, quality of management and staff, or track record). Any firm that's a candidate for a merger or acquisition should meet these criteria before these principals will even consider conducting preliminary negotiations.

They control the process from start to finish. This means they identify all of the firms that meet their basic criteria and establish which of those firms are motivated to sell or merge. Then, instead of dealing with just one firm and hoping they can strike a "win-win" deal, these principals are in a position to speak with multiple firms. This increases their options and allows them significantly more flexibility in negotiations.

Once the integration process is underway, each party should revisit its initial reasons for entering into the transaction, and begin to measure the success of the transaction. This can be done by evaluating the extent to which the deal fulfilled your initial transaction objectives.

It often takes a significant amount of time to be able to measure the success or failure of the transaction. The results can be measured in tangible terms, such as payment of the purchase price and compensation following the closing. Other measures include the preservation of human capital (jobs) and job and career satisfaction and opportunities. In the end, it is some combination of these quantitative and qualitative factors which answer the question of the success or failure of the transaction.

Conclusion

Over the past several years there have been many examples of successful transactions in the A/E/P and environmental consulting industries— the trick is finding the right match, and knowing how to get the most of the deal. Now that we have given you the basics of how to buy or sell a firm, you are ready to begin implementing your strategic plans. Plan carefully, and arm yourself with the best advi-

Preserving Your Identity After the Deal

Figure 10-5

Entrepreneurs start their own A/E/P and environmental consulting firms because they want to call the shots— it's just that simple. So when these principals are faced with the proposition of a merger or an acquisition, it's not uncommon to hear them balk at "being absorbed" or "becoming a puppet."

The owner of a small Boston architectural firm who was recently approached by a national firm for an acquisition put it this way: "I want an acquisition to improve my situation— I'm not interested in becoming absorbed." It's a valid point. But there are examples of small-firm principals who maintained a certain level of authority in the combined entity *after* the deal was done. Here are two.

When 345-person environmental consulting firm **Jacques Whitford Group, Ltd.** (Dartmouth, Nova Scotia) acquired 25-person consulting engineering firm **Robert G. Gerber, Inc.** (Freeport, ME). Robert Gerber, the acquired firm's president, made sure up front that he and his firm would play a prominent role in the new venture. In fact, Gerber is now regional vice president of U.S. Operations and president of a small start-up office in Portland, Maine, that was part of the merger. How did he manage to maintain the autonomy he enjoyed while heading his own firm?

"We negotiated that right away," says Gerber. "It was important to our group to know up front how this was going to work. We started talking in November of 1993, and 15 months later, we consummated the deal— it was a lengthy process."

Gerber says it took time to adequately hammer out the details. "A year is a reasonable amount of time to talk about one of these deals."

He was also careful to document all of his concerns along the way. "Halfway through, we came up with 67 questions we wanted written answers to. We spent a lot of time talking about how we'd work together, where the physical location would be, how the cultures would work together, what the name would be, and who would be doing what jobs. We talked about all of those things— we didn't trust it to fate," he says.

"If a small firm wants to be successful in a merger, they need to get things straightened out up front and get it in writing. A small company won't have a prayer once the merger is done." According to Gerber, his U.S. division did not grow this year, but a potential merger with a 35-person New England-based firm looks promising.

Fred DeFeo, formerly an executive vice president and principal of **DeFeo, Wair and Pare** (Raynham, MA), worked out the details of an acquisition in only 60 days with 180-person environmental consulting firm **Tundra Corp.** (Rockland, MA), and still avoided being "swallowed up." According to David Campbell, Tundra's CEO, DeFeo, Wair and Pare was a $3 million a year operation at the time of the acquisition, yet DeFeo has managed to secure the role of president within the new corporate structure.

The key for small-firm principals who want to keep their identity following a merger or acquisition is to recognize the situation they're in and— as Gerber says— leave nothing to chance.

sors you can find. Understand ahead of time how deals are structured. Conduct a thorough search to provide yourself with a number of choices. Clearly communicate your goals and objectives to potential transaction partners, and listen carefully to what they are looking for from the deal. Take the time to do good research— check and double check areas that are potentially problematic. Listen to your intuition, because if the deal "feels wrong," it probably is. And if it feels right, go for it, but plan to spend some time and energy integrating the firms once all of the paperwork has been signed.

The world of mergers and acquisitions is filled with opportunities— once you know the ropes, you too can join the ranks of firms that have grown, diversified, or transitioned thanks to a merger or acquisition.

For Buyers: Form for Profiling Prospective Sellers

☑ *As a buyer, you will need to gather a great deal of information when you are talking with prospective sellers. This form will help you to collect all of the preliminary information you need.*

FIRM NAME: **DATE:**

Contact Information

Mr./Ms./Dr./_____ First Name:__________________ MI:____________ Last Name:__________________ Suffix:______

Contact Title:____ # years in the position:___________________________

Firm Headquarters

Address:____

City:____ State:__________________ Zip+4:________________________

Phone:_________________________ Fax:__________________________ WWW:___________________________________

Staff Size & Composition

	Full-Time:	Part-Time:	Total:
Number of PEs:			
Number of EITs			
Number of non-registered engineers:			
Number of RLSs:			
Number of AIAs:			
Number of non-registered architects:			
Number of technicians/CADD operators:			
Number of adminstrative staff:			
		Total # of employees:	

Will they send an organizational chart? YES NO

Branch Offices

There are __________ offices, including the HQ office.

Branch Office	City	State	# of employees	Office Manager
1				
2				
3				
4				
5				
6				
7				
8				
9				
10				

Business History & Ownership

When did the business start?____

Who started the business?____

How did it get started? ____

____

____

Business History & Ownership, cont.

Number of owners

If many, list only those who own 5% or more. Ask for a resume for each owner, or a statement of qualifications.

Name	Title	Professional Registration	% Ownership	Employee?

Total % employee ownership:__________ Total % non-employee ownership: __________

Financial Structure

Type of company: ☐ S-Corp ☐ C-Corp ☐ Partnership ☐ Sole Proprietorship ☐ Other __________

Fiscal Year Start:__________ End:__________ Cash or accrual-basis accounting?__________

Small business delegation: ☐ WBE ☐ MBE ☐ DBE ☐ Other __________

Services

Services offered to clients and % of revenues that each contributes to the firm: __________

% of work performed as a prime consultant: __________ % of work performed as a sub consultant:__________

Clients

Types of clients the firm serves and % breakdown of each type of client:__________

% public work: __________ % private work: __________

Technology

Are you computer networked? YES NO Do you have a computer for every person? YES NO

How many computers total?__________

How new is the equipment? __________

What type of WP/spreadsheet software do you use? __________

What type of accounting/project management software do you use?

☐ BST ☐ Timberline ☐ H&S ☐ Other__________

What type of design/drafting software do you use?

☐ AutoCAD Release #__________ ☐ Microstation ☐ Other__________

Project Experience

(For this section, ask the prospective to tell you about three of the firm's recent large or signature projects.)

1. Project name:__________ Location: __________

   Who (or what type of client) was it for?__________

   What was the project?__________

   What was your firm's role in the project?__________

   Start Date: ______ Finish Date: ______ Were you a prime of sub on this project? Prime Sub

   Total project construction cost:______ Firm's fee: ($)______(% of construction costs)______

2. Project name:__________ Location: __________

   Who (what type of client) was it for? __________

   What was the project?__________

   What was your firm's role in the project?__________

   Start Date: ______ Finish Date: ______ Were you a prime of sub on this project? Prime Sub

   Total project construction cost:______ Firm's fee: ($)______(% of construction costs)______

3. Project name:__________ Location: __________

   Who (what type of client) was it for? __________

   What was the project?__________

   What was your firm's role in the project?__________

   Start Date: ______ Finish Date: ______ Were you a prime of sub on this project? Prime Sub

   Total project construction cost:______ Firm's fee: ($)______(% of construction costs)______

Assets

How many company vehicles to you have? __________

What they are used for? __________

Do you own or lease your building?__________

Terms of lease or mortgage:__________

Other assets: __________

____

Professional Liability Insurance

Who is your professional liability carrier *(not local agent)*:

☐ DPIC ☐ CNA ☐ Chinnerer ☐ Other__________

Debt

How many lines of credit do you have?__________

What is the value of each?__________

How much is drawn on each?__________

(Even if they say they don't owe anything, still ask how much their line(s) of credit is for.)

Debt, cont.

What other sources of debt do you have? ____________________

Please describe these sources of debt and what the money is owed for:____________________

____

____

Revenues and Profits

	1996	1995	1994
Gross Revenues			
Net Revenues*			
Pre-tax/Pre-bonus Profit			

**(Net revenues NOT net profit after paying subs.)*
(Gross revenues should be about 100K/head. If the #s are low, double check & ask them to explain.)
(Pre-Tax/Pre-Bonus profits should be about 5-10%; check ups and downs, and ask why they lost money or were profitable.)

What is the book value (total amount of equity) of the firm?____________ As of when?____________

Is this number based on a formula? YES NO

If so, what is the formula?____________________

What are the projected gross revenues for 1997? (or FY 1997 if C-Corp?)____________________

What are the projected pre-tax/pre-bonus profits for 1997? (or FY 1997 if C-Corp?)____________________

Backlog

Please describe your firm's current backlog (work already under contract):____________________

____

(Backlog should be about 6 months to 1 year.)

Motivation To Sell

Why are you interested in selling?____________________

____

What are you looking to do? ☐ Stay: How long? ____________ ☐ Get out?

Have you considered an internal ownership transition (2nd tier)? YES NO

Do you know who your next generation of owners are? YES NO Are they ready? YES NO

If so, why sell? ____________________

____

Have you ever considered a merger or acquisition in the past? YES NO

Have you ever been approached? YES NO

When and by whom?____________________

____

Motivation To Sell, cont.

What happened? Why didn't you pursue? ____________________

____

____

What's different now that you're ready to pursue a transaction? ____________________

____

____

Other Information

How do you think a sale would benefit your firm? ____________________

____

____

What does your firm have to offer an acquiring firm? ____________________

____

____

Additional Notes

For Sellers: Form for Profiling Prospective Buyers

☑ *As a seller, you will need to gather a great deal of information when you are talking with prospective buyers. This form will help you to collect all of the preliminary information you need.*

FIRM NAME: **DATE:**

Contact Information

Mr./Ms./Dr./_____ First Name:__________________ MI:____________ Last Name:__________________ Suffix:______

Contact Title:____

Firm Headquarters

Address:____

City:____ State:_________________ Zip+4:___________________

Phone:_________________________ Fax:_________________________ WWW:_________________________

Acquisition Opportunity

Describe the ideal acquisition opportunity for your firm: _____________________________________

____

____

What is your reason for pursuing this opportunity in particular?______________________________

____

____

What would you consider to be negatives in a deal?____

____

____

Staff Size

Total # of employees: _____________________________

Branch Offices

There are ___________ offices, including the HQ office.

Branch Office	City	State
1		
2		
3		
4		
5		
6		
7		
8		
9		
10		

Revenues and Profits

	1996	1995	1994
Gross Revenues			
Net Revenues*			

**(Net revenues NOT net profit after paying subs.)*

Services

Services offered to clients and % of revenues that each contributes to the firm: ____________________

____

____

Clients

Types of clients the firm serves and % breakdown of each type of client: ____________________

____

____

% public work: ____________________ % private work: ____________________

Business History & Ownership

When did the business start? ____________________

Who started the business? ____________________

How did it get started? ____________________

____

____

Number of owners

If many, list only those who own 5% or more. Ask for a resume for each owner, or a statement of qualifications.

Name	Title	Professional Registration	% Ownership	Employee?

Total % employee ownership: ____________________ Total % non-employee ownership: ____________________

Previous Acquisitions

Please describe any previous acquisitions: ____________________

____

____

____

Other Information

How do you think a merger or acquisition would benefit your firm?

What does your firm have to offer a selling firm?

Additional Notes

Sample Letter of Intent

☑ *Sometimes referred to as a "termsheet" or "memorandum of understanding," the letter of intent is the document that outlines the major points of the transaction.*

XYZ, Inc.
123 High Street
Nowhere, US 01234
(123)456-7890

February 15, 1997

Michael Brown
ABC, Inc.
789 Main Street
Anywhere, US 56789

Dear Mr. Brown:

The purpose of this letter is to set forth the terms of the proposed acquisition by XYZ, Inc. ("XYZ") of certain of the assets [*all the stock*] of ABC, Inc. ("ABC"). The terms of the proposed acquisition are as follows:

1. Purchased Assets

The assets to be acquired include the operating equipment, leasehold improvements, furniture, fixtures and equipment ("Operating Assets"), and the goodwill of ABC, including without limitation client lists, the name "ABC, Inc.", the telephone number (123)456-7890, fax number (123)456-7899, logos, files, records, documents, and other written and recorded materials relating to the operations of ABC ("Goodwill"). (Operating Assets and Goodwill are collectively referred to as "Acquired Assets").

All Acquired Assets shall be conveyed free and clear of all liens, pledges, taxes, encumbrances, restrictions, obligations, and material adverse interests of any kind whatsoever. [*Insert stock here if stock deal.*]

2. Excluded Assets

Excluded from the purchase and sale transaction will be ABC cash, accounts receivable, prepaid taxes, earned revenue in excess of billings, and any amounts due from employees.

XYZ is not purchasing, assuming, or otherwise agreeing to be responsible for any liability of ABC whatsoever, whether now existing or hereafter acquired, including but not limited to accounts payable, notes payable, travel expenses, payroll and insurance accruals, profit sharing accruals, lease obligations through closing, payroll taxes, income taxes, lawsuits, claims or administrative action pending or arising from past or present conduct or ABC, or claims or administrative actions yet to be filed but relating to the pre-closing conduct or action of ABC.

3. Purchase Price/Allocations

The purchase price for the Acquired Assets will be Fifty Thousand Dollars ($50,000) payable in cash. The purchase price will be allocated $45,000 for Operating Assets and $5,000 for Goodwill. [*Insert here if stock and/or promissory notes are being exchanged.*]

4. Employment

XYZ will offer to employ all the current employees of ABC as employees at will, effective as of the Closing.

5. Work-In-Progress; Executory Contracts

ABC will assign to XYZ, as of the Closing, those client contracts and proposals of ABC as to which XYZ has agreed to assume, it being understood that such contracts and proposals either (a) are assignable, or (b) require consent to assignment and such consent will have been obtained.

With respect to such contracts being assumed, XYZ will make a written determination of the percentage of such services completed and billable through the Closing, and XYZ will bill and collect for its own account the services performed and expenses incurred after the Closing.

6. Accounts Receivable

XYZ will provide reasonable assistance to ABC in the collection of the ABC accounts receivable for a period of 120 days after Closing.

7. Lease and Occupancy

XYZ will assume ABC's obligations under the current lease for its premises at 789 Main Street, Anywhere, USA 56789, subject to the consent of the lessor.

8. Conditions Precedent to Closing

This letter setting forth the terms of the purchase of certain assets and certain agreements is subject to ABC's compliance and XYZ's satisfaction with the following list of conditions by way of illustration and not by limitation.

a. Due Diligence Access. From the date of this letter to the Closing, ABC agrees that XYZ may, and its agents, accountants, attorneys, and others, make such investigations of ABC as XYZ may deem necessary or advisable, and ABC will, upon reasonable request, provide such persons with reasonable access to the facilities of ABC and will make available all books, records, data, and other information pertaining to ABC and its respective assets. XYZ may make copies of any such documents and information as it shall determine appropriate.

b. Misrepresentation or Materiality. If during Due Diligence Access XYZ uncovers any information, whether written or verbal, that is different than what has of is presented to it by ABC, its agents, officers, or any other party associated with ABC or if XYZ uncovers information that it feels in its own opinion may affect its ability to compete in the marketplace or perform on future obligations, XYZ at its sole discretion may declare this letter null and void.

c. Definitive Agreements. XYZ and ABC agree to negotiate in good faith and with all due speed the Purchase and Sale Agreement and any other documents necessary to consummate the transaction described herein. The agreements shall incorporate the terms an provisions set forth herein and shall contain such other terms, provisions, representations, warranties, covenants, and conditions as are necessary for transactions of this kind or are as agreed to between XYZ and ABC, including without limitation, a provision by which ABC will indemnify XYZ (a) against any unassumed liabilities, claims, and costs arising out of the conduct of ABC or arising out of any breach or representation, warranty, or covenant made by ABC in the Purchase and Sale Agreement and (b) any third party liability with respect to any ABC contract not assigned to XYZ or otherwise non-assignable.

d. Material Adverse Changes in Business Condition. This letter will become null and void upon any material adverse changes in the assets, financial conditions, personnel or operating performance of ABC. ABC agrees to conduct its business only in the ordinary course.

9. Closing

The Closing of the transaction hereunder shall occur on or before December 31, 1997. XYZ shall have the option to extend the Closing Date to February 28, 1998. The Closing is subject to satisfaction of all conditions set forth herein.

10. Broker

XYZ and ABC each represent and warrant to each other that no broker or other party entitled to a commission or fee is involved in connection with this transaction. ABC agrees to indemnify XYZ against and to hold it harmless from any claim, loss, damage, cost, or liability, including reasonable attorney's fees, incurred as a result of claims for brokerage commissions asserted against XYZ in connection with this transaction. XYZ shall give immediate notice to ABC of any such claim.

11. Fees and Expenses

Each party will bear its own fees and other expenses incurred in connection with this transaction. Each party agrees that in the event of termination, neither party will seek to make a claim for damages, whether actual, compensatory, or punitive.

12. Post Closing Matters

Immediately after the Closing, ABC will proceed diligently to collect its assets and make full payment of all ABC liabilities. It is contemplated that ABC will be liquidated and dissolved promptly.

13. Publicity

It is agreed that no public announcement regarding this letter of the matters contemplated herein will be made until after the Closing.

14. Exclusivity

ABC and its stockholders agree to neither negotiate for nor consummate the sale in any way of any of the assets or equity stock of ABC to any other party from the date hereof until the Closing or until this letter becomes null and void.

15. Non-Binding Effect

This letter is a statement of intention only, is not intended to, and shall not, create a binding legal obligation of any party, and is subject to the approval of the Board of Directors of XYZ, except to the extent of the provisions set forth in paragraphs 10, 11, 13 and 14 hereof, to the satisfactory conclusion of due diligence by XYZ and ABC.

If the foregoing accurately sets forth our mutual understanding, please so indicate by signing below as indicated. If this letter is not accepted and returned to XYZ by November 19, 1997, XYZ may, in its sole discretion, withdraw this offer without notice.

Very truly yours,

XYZ, Inc.

By:________________________________

Agreed as aforesaid:

ABC, Inc.

By:________________________________

ABC Stockholders:

____

____

____

____

____

____

Due Diligence Investigation Checklist

☑ *Being thorough is the key to a successful due diligence search. The best way to make sure that your team conducts a comprehensive investigation that will yield the information you are looking for is to carefully plan out the areas and documents that need to be reviewed.*

Organization and Good Standing

- ☐ Certificate of Incorporation or Articles of Organization, as amended to date
- ☐ By-Laws, as amended to date
- ☐ Good Standing Certificates (long form) and Tax Status Certificates
- ☐ List of states where the Company is (or should be) qualified as a foreign corporation, or has offices (then secure certificates of authority, good standing and tax status certificates)
- ☐ Minutes of the Board of Directors of the Company, including minutes of executive and other committees (board and non-board), from the date of its organization (use these minutes as a cross-check to other items of due diligence)
- ☐ Minutes of the Stockholders of the Company from the date of its organization
- ☐ Partnership or joint venture affiliations
- ☐ Company organization chart showing subsidiaries, if applicable
- ☐ Copies of all press releases relating to the Company from the date of its organization
- ☐ D/B/A certificates
- ☐ List of states where the Company is (or should be) registered with the appropriate board(s) regulating design professionals, and the name of each registered professional

Capitalization and Shareholders

- ☐ List of shareholders, (including position, title, and % ownership of each) cross-checked against stock certificate book; record of other stock issuances
- ☐ Confirmation of no preemptive rights
- ☐ Shareholders' status - minors, trustees, etc.
- ☐ Trust agreements or other documents if shares are held in a fiduciary or entity capacity
- ☐ ESOP, stock bonus or other agreements to issue shares
- ☐ Letter from auditors regarding fully paid and non-assessable character of shares and correct accounting entries
- ☐ If a Subchapter S-corporation, determine validity of elections, and absence of non-qualifying stockholders

- ☐ Stock Restriction and Redemption Agreements. If prior redemption has occurred, determine if stockholders have approved either the agreement or the redemption
- ☐ Consider Power of Attorney and Stock Escrow Agreement
- ☐ Note any buyouts in progress and the status of each

Authorization

- ☐ Review specific authorizing resolutions
- ☐ Consider stockholder approval if partial asset transaction
- ☐ Confirm fiduciary or entity powers to approve
- ☐ Voting trusts, outstanding proxies, or agreements as to voting
- ☐ Restrictive stock transfer agreements (if they exist, confirm prior compliance)

Financial Statements and Other Financial Information

- ☐ Five years consolidated and consolidating statements, with access to auditors and work papers
- ☐ Most recent unaudited statements, with comparable statements for prior year.
- ☐ All projections
- ☐ Direct vs. indirect labor totals (determine multipliers, chargeability, and overhead rates)
- ☐ Gross margin
- ☐ Operating costs and profits
- ☐ Debt-to-equity and return-on-equity ratios
- ☐ Positive or negative return on investment, and salaries and bonuses of shareholders
- ☐ Reimbursable expense markup
- ☐ List major backlog clients and the dollar amount of each project
- ☐ Auditors' letters to management for five years, including all "Memoranda on Accounting Procedures," letters to management relating to internal accounting controls, and management responses
- ☐ Auditors' inquiry letters and replies for five years
- ☐ Arrangements for review by Client's auditors
- ☐ Review of Accounts Receivable (Quality, Aging, Special Cases: list clients and amounts outstanding)
- ☐ Secure credit reports
- ☐ Cost Accounting (Government Contracts); Small business and minority business subcontractors
- ☐ Work in Progress: Note whether or not it is tracked. If it is tracked, note how. Also, list the clients and dollar amounts

Tax Matters

- ☐ Copies of returns for latest closed and all open years (federal, state and local)
- ☐ Audit and revenue agents' reports (federal, state and local)
- ☐ Settlement documents and correspondence for three years

- ☐ Agreements waiving statute of limitations or extending time

Employees, Benefits Plans and Salary Labor Disputes

- ☐ Management and employment agreements; secrecy agreements; change-of-control agreements
- ☐ Pension plans and actuarial reports; confirm current assumptions; IRS determination letters or private letter rulings
- ☐ Profit-sharing plans and agreements; incentive compensation; deferred compensation
- ☐ ESOP and stock bonus plans and arrangements; schedule of options and holders setting forth exercise price and other material terms; schedule as to unfunded liabilities under plans
- ☐ Calculation of liabilities and of fund assets using various assumptions of PBGC
- ☐ Life insurance (including provider, offering requirements, rate, and terms)
- ☐ Short- and long-term disability insurance (including provider and terms)
- ☐ Medical insurance (including provider, outline of available plans, and details for employees with dependents)
- ☐ Dental insurance (including provider and terms)
- ☐ Holidays, vacation days, and sick days
- ☐ Educational assistance and seminar benefits
- ☐ Employee size, turnover, absentee history, distribution.
- ☐ For new key employees, ensure no violation of prior non-competition agreements
- ☐ List of all employees, with titles, function, current compensation and compensation/bonus history
- ☐ Review of all personnel records

Other Contracts and Commitments

- ☐ All loan agreements relating to the indebtedness of the Company (bank loans, notes, revolving credit agreements, indentures, mortgages, trust agreements)
- ☐ Compensating balance arrangements
- ☐ Client lists (maintain special care over this item to prevent use or disclosure if deal falls through)
- ☐ Contract or commitment involving future purchase of materials, supplies, equipment or services
- ☐ Secrecy or non-compete agreements
- ☐ Membership agreements or other relations with trade associations
- ☐ Security agreement (UCC Search by local counsel)
- ☐ Guarantees (affiliates, co-signer of loans, supplier and customer guarantees, credit cards may involve guarantees)
- ☐ Contracts or commitments for charitable or professional contributions
- ☐ Contracts or commitment made out of the ordinary course of business
- ☐ Contracts extending after the closing date

Leases

- ☐ All real property leases
- ☐ Computer and office equipment leases
- ☐ Automobile leases

Personal Property

- ☐ Bills of Sale
- ☐ Liens, security interests, encumbrances (UCC Search)
- ☐ Bank Accounts

Licenses

- ☐ Material license agreements running to and from the Company
- ☐ Software licenses (check number of copies in uses)

Insurance

- ☐ All insurance contracts (property, liability, business interruption, environmental)
- ☐ Key-man insurance
- ☐ Officers and Directors Indemnity Insurance
- ☐ Workers' Compensation. Review past experience
- ☐ List of all claims outstanding under each policy and claims made within past five years
- ☐ Contact Client's carrier regarding continuation of coverage
- ☐ Professional liability insurance

Litigation

- ☐ Complete litigation list
- ☐ Contract local counsel (docket check)
- ☐ Confirm acceptance of insurance coverage
- ☐ Consent decrees and applicable injunctions, etc
- ☐ Pending or threatened proceedings
- ☐ Regulatory Compliance
- ☐ Questionable Payment

Patents and Trademarks

- ☐ Patents list and arrange for patent analysis
- ☐ Trademarks list (confirm continuation notices); service mark list
- ☐ Copyrights List
- ☐ Examine common-law practices

Fixed Assets

- ☐ Autos (note number and how they are depreciated)
- ☐ Building (note location, whether the building is owned or if there are loans outstanding, and appraisal value)

- ☐ Computer hardware and software (note current book value and how depreciated)
- ☐ Furniture and fixtures, including phone system, fax machines, typewriters, etc. (note their current book value and how they are depreciated)
- ☐ Field Equipment (note current book value and how it is depreciated)

Real Properties

- ☐ Deeds
- ☐ Title reports and insurance policies
- ☐ Easements
- ☐ UCC searches in relevant states
- ☐ Zoning regulations or determinations
- ☐ Energy sources and cost
- ☐ All reports on real estate, including all parking areas
- ☐ Depreciation Check (calculate recapture)

Inventory

- ☐ Inventory schedule

Government Regulation; Environmental

- ☐ Reports to and from all regulatory authorities
- ☐ All consents, orders, licenses, permits (occupancy, special permits required for business), approvals, certificates and other authorizations from all regulatory, administrative or governmental agencies, bodies or authorities necessary for the conduct of the Company's business

Access to Books and Records

- ☐ Public and Related Information
- ☐ The Company's annual report to stockholders, quarterly reports, notices of annual or special stockholders' meetings, proxy statements and other communications to the stockholders of the Company and its predecessors for the last five years
- ☐ The Company's and its predecessors' Form 10K, 10Q, and 8-K, Schedule 13-D (filed by the Company and its predecessors, 1933 Act Registration Statements, and any other SEC filings made by the Company or its predecessors for the last five years
- ☐ Officers and Directors questionnaires completed in connection with the Company's most recent proxy statement
- ☐ SEC no-action or other inquiries or comment letters for the last five years
- ☐ All Exhibits to be filed with or incorporated by reference in any Registration Statement and not covered by the foregoing (e.g., instruments defining rights of security holders, letters regarding resignation of director(s), change in accounting principles, etc.)
- ☐ All other documents to be quoted, summarized or cited as a source in any Registration Statement
- ☐ Presentations concerning the Company to security analysts and rating agencies

- [ ] Agreements, if any, relating to subscription for or registration pertaining to the Company's Common Stock now in effect, including any agreements or instruments concerning preemptive rights or affecting the ownership, voting and transfer of stock (including warrants and other to subscribe for securities), and any stand-still or other anti-takeover agreements with third parties currently in effect
- [ ] Any study or report (internal or external) which analyzes or discusses the impact of the Internal Revenue Code of 1986 on the Company

Purchase & Sale Agreement Outline

☑ *The transaction documents, led by the Purchase & Sale Agreement (P&S), supersede all previous written and oral understandings. The P&S outlines and sets forth the basic business deal, and is drawn up by the buyer's attorney.*

(Italicized items indicate provisions which should be included for asset deals and not for stock deals.)

Article I - Sale and Purchase of Shares *(Sale and Purchase of Assets)*

1.1 Sale of Shares *(Sale of Assets)*

1.2 Excluded Assets

1.3 Purchase Price

(a) Purchase Price

(b) Payment of Purchase Price

1.4 Liabilities Assumed

1.5 Excluded Liabilities

1.6 Allocation of Purchase Price

1.7 Purchase Price Adjustment

Article II - Closing

2.1 Time and Place of Closing

2.2 Deliveries at Closing

Article III - Representations and Warranties of the Seller and the Company

3.1 Organization and Qualification

3.2 Subsidiaries; Investments

3.3 Capitalization

3.4 Title to Shares

3.5 Articles of Organization and By-Laws; Minute Books

3.6 Authority

3.7 Absence of Conflict

3.8 Governmental Approvals

3.9 Financial Statements

3.10 No Adverse Change

3.11 Tax Matters

3.12 Compliance with Laws

3.13 Litigation

3.14 Contracts

3.15 Real Property

3.16 Accounts and Notes Receivable

3.17 Inventory

3.18 Personal Property

3.19 Intellectual Property

3.20 Liens

3.21 Indebtedness

3.22 Liabilities

3.23 Suppliers and Customers

3.24 Employment and Labor Agreements

3.25 Employee Benefit Plans

3.26 Employees

3.27 Environmental Matters

3.28 Insurance

3.29 Operations of the Company; Absence of Certain Changes and Events

3.30 Conflicts of Interest

3.31 Books and Records

3.32 Bank Accounts

3.33 Brokers

3.34 Full Disclosure

Article IV - Representations and Warranties of Buyer

4.1 Organization

4.2 Authority

4.3 Absence of Conflicts

4.4 Brokers

4.5 Purchase for Investment

4.6 Full Disclosure

Article V - Covenants and Agreements of Selling Stockholders and the Company

5.1 Conduct of Business

5.2 Insurance

5.3 Litigation

5.4 Continued Effectiveness of Representations and Warranties

5.5 Advice of Changes

5.6 Access to Information; Confidentiality

5.7 No Solicitation

5.8 Further Assurances

Article VI - Conditions Precedent to the Obligations of Buyer to Close

6.1 Representations and Covenants

6.2 Governmental Permits and Approvals

6.3 Legal Proceedings

6.4 Environmental Reports

6.5 Third Party Consents

6.6 Financial Condition

6.7 Consulting, Employment and Non-Competition Agreements

6.8 Lease

6.9 Escrow Agreement

6.10 Opinion of Seller's Counsel

Article VII - Conditions Precedent to Company and Seller's Obligations to Close

7.1 Representations and Covenants

7.2 Governmental Permits and Authority

7.3 Legal Proceedings

7.4 Consulting, Employment and Non-Competition Agreements

7.5 Lease

7.6 Escrow Agreement

7.7 Opinion of Buyer's Counsel

Article VIII - Indemnification

8.1 Indemnification by Seller

8.2 Indemnification by Buyer

8.3 Notice and Opportunity to Defend

8.4 Survival of Representations and Warranties

8.5 Limitation on Indemnification

8.6 Recoveries, Payment of Losses, Right of Set-Off

Article IX - Termination of Agreement

9.1 Termination of Agreement

9.2 Procedure for and Effect of Termination

Article X - Miscellaneous

10.1 Fees and Expenses

10.2 Publicity; Public Announcements

10.3 Notices

10.4 Entire Agreement

10.5 Bulk Sales

10.6 Waivers and Amendments

10.7 Assignment

10.8 Counterparts

10.9 Headings

10.10 Severability

10.11 Governing Law

10.12 Exhibits and Schedules

EXHIBITS

Exhibit A - Form of Employment Agreement

Exhibit B - Form of Consulting Agreement

Exhibit C - Form of Non-Competition Agreement

Exhibit D - Form of Escrow Agreement

Exhibit F - Form of Opinion of Seller's Counsel

Exhibit G - Form of Opinion of Buyer's Counsel

SCHEDULES

3.1 Jurisdiction where Company is Qualified to do Business

3.2 Subsidiaries; Jurisdiction of Incorporation and where Qualified to do Business

3.7 Conflicts

3.8 Permits

3.11 Tax Matters

3.12 Compliance with Law

3.13 Litigation

3.14 Contracts

3.15 Real Property

3.16 Accounts Receivable

3.17 Inventory

3.18 Personal Property

3.19 Intellectual Property

3.20 Liens

3.21 Indebtedness

3.22 Liabilities

3.23 Suppliers and Clients

3.24 Employment and Labor Matters

3.25 Employment Benefit Plans

3.26 Employees

3.27 Environmental Matters

3.28 Insurance

3.30 Conflicts of Interest

3.32 Bank Accounts

Stockholders' Agreement Outline

☑ *The following is an outline of a Stockholders' Agreement, including the alternative scenarios that may ensue.*

This agreement applies to all current stockholders and all persons who become stockholders.

A. Restrictions on Transfer

- No transfers or pledges are allowed, except in accordance with the agreement.

Alternative 1: *The transfer restriction may be waived by 75% of the Board of Directors*
Alternative 2: Allow transfer of stock to familial members and/or family trusts.

B. Events Triggering Total Redemption of Stock

- Death.
- Disability.
- Bankruptcy.
- Assignment for the benefit of creditors.
- Termination of employment for any reason.
- Violation of Transfer Restrictions.

Alternative: *Part-time Employment. Under age X and works less than 40 hours per week over a six month period. X or over but less than Y and works less than 20 hours per week over a six month period.*

Alternative to B.: Events Triggering Gradual Redemption of Stock.

- *Gradual redemption commencing at age X, continuing for Z years. (Stockholder may have retired or continues to be actively employed.)*

C. Purchase Price

- Net Book Value, Net Book Value plus Goodwill Factor.

Alternative 1: *Net Book Value, adjusted (except in the case of death) to reflect (i) estimate of collectability of accounts receivable, (ii) review of percentage of work completed for jobs in progress and a reconciliation of same with billings related thereto, (iii) review of all pending and threatened lawsuits and claims, (iv) review of potential uninsured liabilities, (v) amortization of leasehold improvements, (vi) exclusion of any life insurance payable to the Corporation.*

Alternative 2: *Reduction of purchase price by x% if stockholder voluntarily terminates employment prior to scheduled retirement (except for death) or is terminated "for cause."*

D. Purchase Methods and Payment Terms

- Cross-purchase (purchase by other stockholders).
- Single Cash Payment by the Corporation.
- Installments from the Corporation monthly over [*5 to 10*] years, with a low interest factor.

Alternative: *The length of time can be a variable depending upon the reason for the redemption. Scheduled retirement (full or partial) can have a shorter payment period than in the case of voluntary termination before retirement or termination for cause.*

E. Repurchase Upon Death

- The Corporation may purchase life insurance on the lives of stockholders. In the event of redemption upon death, the life insurance proceeds, up to the purchase price, will be paid to the estate. If a balance remains, the balance will be paid pursuant to installment payments. If the insurance proceeds exceed the purchase price, the corporation retains such excess.

F. Legended Stock

- Legend of restrictions on stock certificates.

G. Dispute Resolution

- Mandatory arbitration.

H. Maximum Annual Redemption Payments

- The Corporation will not pay out more than *x*% of annual net income after fair compensation to principals in any one year toward the redemption of stock. If such amount is insufficient to pay all installments due in such year, then the allowed payment will be paid *pro rata* to the former stockholders due payments in such year, and the unpaid amount will be deferred to the next year.

I. Non-Solicitation Covenants

- Upon termination of employment, a stockholder agrees not to solicit any current client (client of corporation within one year of termination) or any employee of Corporation for [*6-12*] months.

J. Covenants of Stockholders

- Determine if any actions require a super majority vote.
- Proprietary and Confidential Information
- Defense of Claims
- Each stockholder will cooperate with the Corporation with respect to any claim or lawsuit against the Corporation.

M&A Transactions in the A/E/P and Environmental Consulting Industries

☑ *The following is a chronological sampling (taken from Zweig White & Associates' Merger & Acquisition Advisor) of the many mergers, acquisitions, and consolidations that have taken place in the A/E/P and environmental consulting industries over the past few years.*

January 1994

Rust Environmental & Infrastructure (Birmingham, AL) acquired **Wahler Associates** (Palo Alto, CA).

April 1994

JBM Engineers and Planners, Inc. (Kansas City, MO), a 141-person consulting engineering firm, acquired **Triton Consulting, Inc.** (Schaumberg, IL), a 30-person consulting engineering firm on April 26.

June 1994

Trow Consulting Engineers (Brampton, Ontario) sold its Boston-area construction materials testing and engineering operation to **Engitek, Inc.** (Cranston, RI).

JBM Engineers and Planners, Inc. (Kansas City, MO), a 171-person consulting engineering firm, acquired the Des Moines, Iowa, office of **Anderson-Bogert, Inc.** (Cedar Rapids, IA), a 17-person consulting engineering firm.

Armour Cape & Pond, Inc. (Atlanta, GA), a 60-person engineering and architecture firm, acquired **Nash M. Love & Associates** (Springfield, VA), a 12-person engineering firm.

Dames & Moore (Los Angeles, CA), a 2,000-person environmental firm, acquired **Balsam Environmental Consultants, Inc.** (Salem, NH), a 60-person environmental consulting firm in an all-cash transaction.

Kleinfelder, Inc. (Walnut Creek, CA), a 650-person environmental consulting firm, acquired **OP&L, Inc.** (San Diego, CA), a three-person environmental consulting firm specializing in air quality and hazardous waste issues.

Rust Environmental & Infrastructure (Birmingham, AL) acquired **Lichliter Jameson & Associates** (Houston, TX), a 200-person consulting engineering and planning firm.

Michael Baker Corp. (Pittsburgh, PA) completed the sale of **Weston Geophysical Corp.** (Westboro, MA) to **Geophex Ltd.** (Raleigh, NC).

July 1994

Groundwater Technology, Inc. (Norwood, MA), a 1,500-person environmental firm, acquired **Hall Southwest Corp.** (Austin, TX), a 40-person environmental firm. Under the terms of the acquisition, Doug Hall, founder and president of Hall Southwest, became general manager in the southwest for GTI's National Industry Division.

Harding Associates, Inc. (Novato, CA), a 1,000-person consulting engineering and environmental firm, acquired the assets of **Alpha Engineering Group, Inc.** (Bellevue, WA), a 150-person consulting engineering firm. The transaction was accounted for as a purchase.

EMCON (San Mateo, CA), a 950-person environmental consulting firm, announced the completion of its acquisition of **Wehran Envirotech, Inc.** (Middletown, NY), a 250-person environmental consulting firm. Under the agreement, Wehran became a wholly-owned subsidiary of EMCON operating as an autonomous unit within the EMCON organization.

R.A. Smith & Associates (Brookfield, WI), a 70-person consulting engineering and environmental firm acquired **National Survey & Engineering, Inc.** (Brookfield, WI), a 45-person consulting engineering firm. Jim Haertel, controller at R.A. Smith, said the deal combined one firm (Smith) doing a large percentage of public work with one (NS&E) that dealt almost totally in private projects. NS&E continued to operate under that name, but formally became a division of R.A. Smith.

August 1994

A joint venture of **Hellmuth Obata & Kassabaum (HOK), Inc.** (St. Louis, MO) and **Kajima International** (Englewood Cliffs, NJ) added a third element when it acquired 50-person environmental consulting firm **Qsource** (Miamisburg, OH). Mike Mariscalco, former president of Qsource, became the president and CEO of HOK/K Industrial.

Shield Environmental Associates (Charlotte, NC), a 65-person environmental consulting firm, acquired the assets of the Lexington, Kentucky, office of 26-person environmental consulting firm **Hatcher-Sayre, Inc.** (Richmond, VA). James Knauss, who managed the office for Hatcher-Sayre, actually acquired the office from Hatcher-Sayre, then sold it to Shield in a stock swap. He became a principal of Shield and continued to head that office.

EARTH TECH (Long Beach, CA), a 1,500-person environmental firm, acquired 300-employee remediation contractor **HazWaste Industries, Inc.** (Richmond, VA) in a stock swap. The deal improved the company's full-service capabilities. HazWaste Industries became a wholly-owned subsidiary of Earth Tech.

September 1994

JBM Engineers & Planners, Inc. (Kansas City, MO), a 135-person consulting engineering firm, acquired 35-person **Everage Consultants, Inc.** (Fort Worth, TX).

Converse Consultants Southwest, Inc. (Las Vegas, NV), a 50-person environmental consulting and materials testing firm, acquired **EssTek, Inc.** (Englewood, CO), a 15-person environmental management firm. Converse planned to change EssTek's name to Converse Consultants MR, Inc., with the MR standing for "Mountain Region."

October 1994

Environmental consulting firm **Dames & Moore** (Los Angeles, CA) completed an all-cash transaction to acquire the shares of **Bureau Voor Milieumanagement (BVM)** (The Hague, Netherlands), a privately held, 18-person environmental consulting firm.

November 1994

Ammann and Whitney (New York, NY), a 250-person bridge design firm with offices in six states, merged with **The Berger Group** (East Orange, NJ), a multidiscipline design and consulting organization that included **Louis Berger International** (East Orange, NJ). Ammann and Whitney continued to operate under its own management and retained its name.

Bucher, Willis & Ratliff (BWR) (Salina, KS), a 225-person A/E firm, acquired six-person architectural firm **Moyes Associates, Ltd.** (Boulder, CO). BWR integrated the Moyes office into its Denver office.

Environmental Services of America, Inc. (ENSA) (Newark, NJ) acquired the assets of 55-person environmental consulting firm **Earth Science Technologies, Inc.** (Louisville, KY). Jody Zimmerman, Earth Science's founder and former president, became a regional vice president for the newly formed **ENSA Environmental, Inc.** (Doylestown, PA).

Karlsberger Companies (Columbus, OH) acquired 10-employee architecture firm **Garikes Wilson & Associates** (Birmingham, AL). The acquired firm changed its name to "Garikes Wilson Karlsberger" on December 1, and its principals remained with the firm.

December 1994

CON-TEST, Inc. (East Longmeadow, MA), a 170-employee environmental consulting firm, was purchased by 500-person environmental consulting firm **ATC Environmental, Inc.** (New York, NY), a publicly-traded company. The price was \$3.735 million, including a \$2.1 million cash down payment. Of the remaining amount, \$1.1 million was in approximately 117,000 restricted common shares of ATC stock, and \$535,000 was in a three-year promissory note. In addition, ATC assumed \$3.5 million of trade accounts payable, notes payable, accrued liabilities, and long-term debt.

Normandeau Associates (Bedford, NH), a 130-person environmental consulting firm, acquired all the assets of the consulting and laboratory divisions of **RMC Environmental Services, Inc.** (Spring City, PA), a 150-person environmental firm. The purchase price was \$5.5 million, plus assumption of certain liabilities. The 110-person consulting arm of the firm became RMC Environmental Services, a division of Normandeau Associates. The 40-person laboratory division became part of **Thermo Analytical** (Waltham, MA), which, like Normandeau Associates, is a division of **Thermo Process Systems, Inc.** (Waltham, MA).

Carter & Burgess, Inc. (Fort Worth, TX), a 700-person E/A firm, acquired the Phoenix, Arizona, and Irvine, California, offices of CRSS Civil Engineers from **Jacobs Engineering Group, Inc.** (Pasadena, CA).

Kimley-Horn & Associates, Inc. (Raleigh, NC), a 500-person consulting engineering and environmental consulting firm, acquired 28-person environmental consulting firm **Rady & Associates, Inc.** (Fort Worth, TX).

January 1995

GEI Consultants, Inc. (Winchester, MA), a 200-person consulting engineering firm, acquired 30-person geotechnical firm **Roger Foott & Associates** (San Francisco, CA). The deal gave GEI a stronger presence in Southern California and expanded its geotechnical capabilities.

February 1995

URS Corporation (San Francisco, CA), a 1,300-person E/A firm, acquired 50-person transportation design firm **E.C. Driver & Associates** (Tallahassee, FL). The acquisition allowed URS to strategically expand in the growing transportation infrastructure market.

Radian Corp. (Austin, TX), a 2,000-person environmental consulting firm, acquired a controlling interest in **Pacific Peregren, Inc.** (Redwood City, CA), a 16-person remediation firm. The name "Pacific Peregren, Inc." was changed to Radian D-Tech. Mark DeMent, former president of Pacific Peregren, became president of the new entity. The deal gave Radian expanded capabilities in a number of remediation-related areas.

Science Applications International Corp. (SAIC) (La Jolla, CA), an 18,000-person consulting engineering and environmental consulting firm, acquired **R.E. Wright Associates, Inc.** (Middletown, PA), and its two sister firms **Environmental Restorations Systems, Inc.** (Middletown, PA) and **Wright Lab Services, Inc.** (Middletown, PA). Richard E. Wright continued to serve as president of the three Wright companies.

Harza Engineers & Scientists (Oakland, CA), a 50-person subsidiary of 900-person consulting engineering firm **Harza Engineering Company** (Chicago, IL), acquired seven-person seismic risk and earthquake engineering analysis firm **Lindvall Richter Benuska Associates** (Los Angeles, CA). The acquired firm changed its name to Harza/LRB.

March 1995

Groundwater Technology, Inc. (GTI) (Norwood, MA), a 1,600-person environmental consulting, engineering, and remediation firm, acquired the 60-person Hazardous Waste Division of **Chester Environmental, Inc.** (Pittsburgh, PA). The acquired division became a large part of GTI's National Industry Division, and became its Pittsburgh hub of operations.

Two transportation firms prominent in New York, New Jersey and the Middle Atlantic states joined together. **SITE Engineers, Inc.** (Mt. Laurel, NJ), a 200-person consulting engineering firm, acquired **Blauvelt Engineers, P.C.** (New York, NY), a 50-person consulting engineering firm, and the combined firm became SITE-Blauvelt Engineers.

RMT, Inc. (Madison, WI), a 500-person environmental consulting firm, acquired 20-person environmental consulting firm **Braithwaite Consultants** (Ann Arbor, MI).

April 1995

CTL/Thompson (Denver, CO), a 150-person geotechnical firm, acquired **Patton & Burke, Inc.** (Dallas, TX), an 8-person geotechnical firm. The move was designed to make CTL/Thompson a more regional force in the geotechnical market. The Dallas firm was renamed Patton, Burke & Thompson.

Park Environmental Corp. (Anaheim, CA), a 200-person environmental consulting firm, acquired **GHH Environmental** (Citrus Heights, CA), a 20-person environmental consulting firm. GHH became a branch office of Park Environmental.

May 1995

Carter & Burgess, Inc. (Ft. Worth, TX), a 750-person full-service E/A/P firm, acquired **MEA, Inc.** (Las Vegas, NV), a 20-person consulting engineering and surveying firm. The deal increased C&B's presence in Las Vegas. MEA's office continued to operate separately from C&B's project office in Las Vegas, but its name was changed to Carter & Burgess.

Woodward-Clyde Group, Inc. (Denver, CO), a 2,800-person environmental consulting firm, entered the construction business by acquiring **Geo-Con, Inc.** (Monroeville, PA), one of the nations largest specialty contractors. The transaction was an attempt by Woodward-Clyde to capitalize on the growing popularity of design-build.

OHM Corporation (Findlay, OH), a 3,100-employee environmental remediation firm, and 23,000-employee environmental consulting and remediation firm **Rust International, Inc.** (Birmingham, AL) completed the merger of Rust's hazardous waste and nuclear waste remediation business into OHM. Under the agreement, 9,668,000 shares of OHM common stock were issued to Rust, a majority-owned subsidiary of **WMX Technologies** (Oak Brook, IL) in exchange for the businesses received. Cash received by OHM at the closing was used to reduce amounts outstanding under the company's revolving credit facility. Additionally, in exchange for WMX's agreement to provide a credit enhancement, OHM also issued a warrant to WMX to purchase 700,000 shares of OHM common stock at $15 per share, exercisable over five years.

June 1995

Carter & Burgess, Inc. (Ft. Worth, TX), a 750-person full-service E/A/P firm, and **RNL Facilities Corporation** (Denver, CO), a 100-person A/E firm, formed the **Maintenance Design Group (MDG)** (Denver, CO), a wholly owned venture of the two firms.

DSAtlantic Corp. (Raleigh, NC), a 175-employee E/A firm, acquired **American Engineers** (Richmond, VA), a 40-employee transportation engineering firm. The acquired firm took the DSAtlantic name, and its Raleigh branch office consolidated into the acquiring firm's Richmond office.

July 1995

Galston Corporation (East Syracuse, NY), a 350-employee environmental consulting firm, acquired 60-employee A/E firm **Lozier Architects & Engineers** (Pittsford, NY).

Flour Daniel (Irvine, CA), a 4,500-employee engineering/construction firm, acquired a majority interested in **Prosynchem** (Gliwice, Poland), a full-service engineering and construction services firm.

Four firms created a limited liability company— **Nevada Testing and Technology, LLC** (Las Vegas, NV)— in order to pursue the U.S. Department of Energy's (DOE) Management and Operating contract at the Nevada Test Site. The four firms involved were **Holmes & Narver** (Orange, CA), **Parsons Brinkerhoff** (New York, NY), **E-Systems** (Springfield, VA), and **Foster Wheeler Corp.** (Clinton, NJ).

Raytheon Engineers & Constructors (Lexington, MA), a 15,000-employee engineering and construction firm, completed the purchase of the assets of 900-employee **Litwin Engineers & Constructors** (Houston, TX), the engineering and construction subsidiary of **United Dominion Industries Limited** (Charlotte, NC).

August 1995

The 290-employee A/E firm **ADP/Fluor Daniel** (Tucson, AZ) acquired 11-employee architecture firm **Allen & Philip** (Phoenix, AZ). The firms planned to merge Allen & Philip's office with the Phoenix office of ADP/Fluor Daniel and call it ADP/Allen & Philip (Phoenix, AZ).

Post, Buckley, Schuh & Jernigan (Miami, FL), a 1,300-employee E/A firm, acquired 90-employee land planning, engineering and surveying firm **The Nelson Corp.** (Dallas, TX).

ICF Kaiser International, Inc. (Fairfax, VA), a 5,700-employee environmental engineering and consulting firm, acquired four-person consulting firm **Rankin Environmental Group** (Arlington, VA).

NYTEST Environmental, Inc. (Port Washington, NY) acquired the laboratory division of the former **BCM Engineers, Inc.** (Plymouth Meeting, PA) from **Smith Environmental Technologies, Inc.** (Dallas, TX). The lab became a wholly owned subsidiary of **NYTEST, NEI of Pennsylvania** (Norristown, PA).

ENVIROMETRICS, Inc. (Charleston, SC), a holding company for environmental, health, and analytical laboratories companies, acquired the assets of the environmental air monitoring business from the Nuclepore Division of **Corning Costar Corp.**, a division of **Corning, Inc.**

September 1995

Stecker LaBau Arneill McManus Architects, Inc. (Glastonbury, CT) merged with **Russell Gibson von Dohlen, Inc.** (Farmington, CT) to form 135-person A/E firm **The SLAM Collaborative** (Glastonbury, CT).

Clayton Environmental Consultants (Novi, MI), a 500-employee full-service environmental, health, and safety consulting and analytical laboratory company, acquired 90-person consulting and remediation firm **Mittelhauser Corp.** (Chicago, IL), and **HAZCON, Inc.** (Seattle, WA), a 60-person provider of industrial hygiene, safety, and training services.

October 1995

Perkins & Will (Chicago, IL), a 275-person A/E firm, acquired 100-person architectural firm **Nix Mann & Associates** (Atlanta, GA). On October 30, the Atlanta firm began operating as Nix Mann/Perkins & Will.

November 1995

Three mid-sized firms merged to form **TranSystems Corporation** (Kansas City, MO). **JBM Engineers & Planners, Inc.** (Kansas City, MO) joined **Boyd Brown Stude & Cambern (BBSC)** (Kansas City, MO) and **Vickerman Zachary Miller (VZM)** (Oakland, CA) to establish the new venture. Each firm became a separate operating division of TranSystems Corporation.

December 1995

Goodkind & O'Dea (Rutherford, NJ), a 265-person consulting engineering firm, acquired 15-person consulting engineering firm **Genovese & Associates** (Woodbridge, CT). Goodkind & O'Dea, a subsidiary of **Dewberry & Davis, Inc.** (Fairfax, VA), moved its 20-person North Haven, Connecticut, office into Genovese's facilities and changed the branch name to "Goodkind & O'Dea/Genovese."

Henneman Raufeisen and Associates, Inc. (Champaign, IL), a 40-person E/A/P firm, merged with 20-person mechanical/electrical firm **S & R Engineering, Inc.** (Urbana, IL). The combined firm retained the Henneman Raufeisen name because the 35-year-old firm had more name recognition than its 18-year-old counterpart.

January 1996

Kennedy/Jenks Consultants, Inc. (San Francisco, CA), a 275-person consulting engineering firm, acquired **Ricks Taylor & Associates** (Bakersfield, CA), a 5-person consulting engineering firm.

Core Laboratories (Houston, TX) bought four environmental testing labs from **Pace, Inc.** (Minneapolis, MN).

David Evans & Associates (DEA), Inc. (Portland, OR), a 600-person E/A firm, recently acquired nine-person architecture firm **Jamie Cannon & Associates** (St. Louis, MO) and four-person planning firm **Tierra Planning & Design** (San Juan Capistrano, CA). Both firms retained their previous names, but added a suffix identifying them as "A David Evans & Associates Company."

On January 2, **NYTEST Environmental, Inc.** (Port Washington, NY) announced that it completed the acquisition of 150-person **GTEL Environmental Laboratories** (Milford, NH). GTEL was a former subsidiary of **Groundwater Technology, Inc.** (Norwood, MA), 1,600-person environmental consulting firm.

February 1996

The Ratcliff Architects (Emeryville, CA), a 50-person architecture and planning firm, merged with 25-person planning, architecture, and interior design firm **Crosby Helmich Architects** (San Francisco, CA). The merged firm took the 90-year-old Ratcliff name.

Philip Environmental, Inc. (Hamilton, Ontario) acquired the laboratory division of **Zenon Environmental, Inc.** (Burlington, Ontario) for $7.5 million (Canadian). The deal was for $7 million in cash and $500,000 in assumed liabilities.

Earth Search Sciences (McCall, ID), a 15-person publicly traded holding company, acquired **Lamb Associates, Inc. (LAI)** (Rockville, MD), a 125-person consulting engineering and technical services firm, for $2.5 million in cash and stocks.

March 1996

Golder Associates Corp. (Atlanta, GA), a 1,500-person environmental consulting firm, and **KBN Engineering and Applied Sciences, Inc.** (Gainesville, GA), a 100-person air quality services provider, merged. Both firms were employee owned.

International Technology Corp.(Torrance, CA), a 2,500-person environmental management firm, acquired **Gradient Corp.** (Cambridge, MA), a 100-person environmental consulting firm.

TranSystems Corporation (Kansas City, MO), a 325-person engineering, architecture, and planning firm, sold its Des Moines, Iowa, branch office. The buyer was the former manager of the office, Douglas Saltsgaver, who became the president of the new firm, **Engineering Resource Group, Inc.** (Des Moines, IA).

April 1996

URS Corporation (San Francisco, CA) completed its acquisition of **Greiner Engineering, Inc.** (Irving, TX) on April 1. The acquisition of Greiner gave URS a full national presence with more than 60 domestic offices, and aided URS in its efforts to explore opportunities in the Pacific Rim. The acquisition was accomplished through the issuance of $13.50 per share in cash and .298 shares of URS common stock for every common share of Greiner. Based on Greiner's 4,704,642 outstanding shares of common stock, the aggregate consideration was approximately $63.5 million in cash and 1.4 million shares of URS common stock. To finance the acquisition, URS entered into a new $70 million secured credit facility with Wells Fargo Bank, N.A.

Tyco International (Exeter, NH) completed the acquisitions of **Whitman & Howard, Inc.** (Wellesley, MA) and **Barrett Consulting Group** (Menlo Park, CA) and combined the firms with its **EARTH TECH** (Long Beach, CA) division.

Nolte & Associates, Inc. (Walnut Creek, CA), a 260-person consulting engineering firm, purchased selected assets of railway engineering specialist **Summit/Lynch Consulting Engineers, Inc.** (Reno, NV). The purchase was made from **Summit Engineering Corp.** (Reno, NV).

Fluor Daniel, Inc. (Irvine, CA) acquired ownership of British maintenance, consulting, and manpower services company **T.A. Group Ltd.** (Farnham, UK). T.A. continued to operated independently as a wholly owned subsidiary of Fluor Daniel.

May 1996

The Sear-Brown Group (Rochester, NY), a 350-person multidiscipline E/A firm merged with **RBD, Inc.** (Fort Collins, CO), a 60-person environmental consulting firm.

Fluor Daniel Environmental Services, Inc. (Irvine, CA), a 200-person subsidiary of **Fluor Daniel, Inc.** (Irvine, CA), completed its merger with **Groundwater Technology, Inc.** (Norwood, MA). The new firm is 1,450-person **Fluor Daniel GTI** (Norwood, MA). Fluor Daniel acquired 4.4 million shares, or approximately 55% interest in GTI. Fluor Daniel contributed $33.35 million in cash and ownership of its subsidiary, Fluor Daniel Environmental Services, to the company. GTI shareholders exchanged their shares for approximately $60 million in cash and 45% ownership of Fluor Daniel GTI.

June 1996

ATC Environmental, Inc. (New York, NY) acquired certain assets of 1,000-person environmental consulting firm **ATEC Associates** (Indianapolis, IN). ATC paid $15 million for the firm, and agreed to pay contingent considerations of as much as $10.75 million if certain revenue targets were achieved.

Towill, Inc. (San Francisco, CA), a 70-person aerial mapping and surveying firm, acquired selected assets of two small California firms— 18-person **Coast Surveying, Inc.** (Irvine, CA) and **Zenith Aerial Mapping** (Carlsbad, CA).

Stanley Technologies Group, Inc. (Edmonton, Alberta), a consulting engineering, planning, management, and scientific firm, acquired the operating assets of transportation, urban development, and environmental engineering firm **DWL Engineering, Inc.** (Calgary, Alberta).

The Pace Corporation (Toronto, Ontario), an international developer, manufacturer, and distributor of medical and environmental test kits, acquired lead testing and remediation firm **Ramsey-Schilling Consulting Group** (Kansas City, MO). It was agreed that the acquisition would be paid for over a two-year period in cash and shares of Pace.

Fluor Daniel Pty. Ltd. (Melbourne, Australia), a subsidiary of **Fluor Daniel, Inc.** (Irvine, CA), acquired **Signet Engineering Group** (Melbourne, Australia), a privately owned engineering firm.

July 1996

Thielsch Engineering (Cranston, RI), a 150-person, consulting engineering, inspection, and lab services firm, acquired 25-person analytical laboratory **ESS Laboratory** (Providence, RI) from **Environmental Science Services, Inc.** (Providence, RI).

Evans Environmental Corp. (Miami, FL) completed the acquisition of all issued and outstanding stock of **American Remedial Technologies, Inc. (ART)** (Miami, FL). Evans paid ART's founder and sole shareholder Enrique Tomeu $6 million in cash, 3 million shares of Evans' common stock, and 1 million shares of its Series B preferred stock.

Allstate GeoTek (Linden, NJ), an environmental service firm, acquired **Zecco, Inc.** (Northborough, MA), an environmental consulting and laboratory firm.

Day & Zimmerman International, Inc. (Philadelphia, PA) and **Environmental Science & Engineering, Inc. (ESE)** (Peoria, IL) established a new environmental remediation company, **DSE Environmental, LLC** (Philadelphia, PA). D&Z and ESE were equal partners in the new firm, but maintained separate corporate identities and business activities.

August 1996

Symmes Maini & McKee Associates, Inc. (Cambridge, MA) acquired 40-person architectural firm **Winsor/Faricy Architects** (St. Paul, MN), which brought the A/E firm's total number of employees to more than 200.

The Failure Group (Menlo Park, CA), a holding company for environmental consulting firm **Failure Analysis Associates, Inc.** (Menlo Park, CA) acquired **Environmental Health Strategies, Inc. (EHS)** (Redwood City, CA), which specialized in environmental studies used for safety and risk management, product and facility design, failure analysis, and litigation support.

Enron Corp. (Houston, TX), a natural gas company, merged with **Portland General Corp.** (Portland, OR) in a tax-free, stock-for-stock transaction.

September 1996

The Stichler Design Group, Inc. (San Diego, CA), a 100-person A/E and construction management firm, acquired 10-person architectural firm **Turley Beck Architects, Ltd.** (Phoenix, AZ). The acquisition was designed to strengthen Stichler's base in the Southwest and provide the firm with a new industry specialty.

The Presnell Group (Louisville, KY), a 130-person E/A, environmental, and construction management firm, acquired 25-person, interior design firm **RDA International, Inc.** (Atlanta, GA).

Dudek & Associates, Inc. (Encinitas, CA), a 90-person environmental consulting and consulting engineering firm, acquired 4-person **J. Harlan Glenn & Associates, Inc.** (Orange, CA), which specialized in special water projects. The selling firm retained its name, operating as a division of Dudek & Associates.

Mid-State Associates, Inc. (Baraboo, WI), a 200-person environmental consulting firm, sold its 20-person laboratory services division to 110-person lab firm **Commonwealth Technology, Inc.** (Lexington, KY).

David Evans & Associates (DEA), Inc. (Portland, OR) acquired 20-person land development, planning, and surveying firm **Bryan & Murphy Associates, Inc.** (San Ramon, CA). The selling firm was a 50-year-old company with an established reputation in the San Francisco Bay Area. DEA made the acquisition to strengthen its position in that region and to acquire the talents of Bryan & Murphy principal Rich Gorman.

Van Cleef Engineering Associates (Belle Mead, NJ) merged 35-person consulting engineering firm **Johnson Engineering, Inc.** (Morristown, NJ) into its operations. Johnson maintained its staff and operations in Morristown, operating as the northern branch of 110-person consulting engineering and surveying firm Van Cleef Engineering.

October 1996

PSI (Lawrence, KS), a 3,000-person environmental consulting, geotechnical engineering, and construction testing firm, acquired 42-person geotechnical and construction materials testing firm **Geo Design Consultants, Inc.** (Virginia Beach, VA).

Crafton, Tull & Associates (CTA), Inc. (Rogers, AR), a 75-person A/E firm, acquired **Mansur-Daubert-Strella (MDS)** (Tulsa, OK), a 16-person civil engineering firm.

November 1996

S E A Consultants, Inc. (Cambridge, MA), a 100-person E/A firm, acquired **Caron Engineering, Inc.** (Concord, NH), a 10-person civil, structural, and traffic engineering firm

Brown, Vence & Associates, Inc. (BVA) (San Francisco, CA), a 50-employee waste management and energy consulting firm, acquired three solid waste specialty firms: **Dilip Patel & Associates (DPA)** (Los Alamitos, CA), **3E Engineering** (Freemont, CA), and **Solution Resources, Inc.** (Grass Valley, CA).

The 25-person firm **Michaels Engineering, Inc. (MEI)** (LaCrosse, WI) merged with 5-person **Chris C. Olson Engineers (CCOE)** (LaCrosse, WI). The firm changed its name to Michaels Engineering.

Jellinek, Schwartz & Connolly, Inc. (JSC) (Arlington, VA), a 75-person environmental consulting firm, acquired 6-person firm **Sielken, Inc.** (Bryan, TX). Sielken continued to operate as a wholly owned subsidiary of JSC and added statistical analysis to JSC's environmental science, policy, and management capabilities.

Petrocon Engineering, Inc. (Beaumont, TX), a 1,500-person engineering/construction firm, acquired 1,000-person engineering and construction firm **RPM Engineering, Inc.** (Baton Rouge, LA).

December 1996

Dewberry & Davis, Inc. (Fairfax, VA), a 1,200-person A/E/P firm, completed its acquisition of 90-person A/E firm **HTB, Inc.** (Oklahoma City, OK). It was agreed that the acquired firm's offices in Oklahoma City and Tulsa would operate as a division of Dewberry & Davis' architectural division, **Dewberry & Davis Design Group** (Fairfax, VA).

JKB&B (Columbia, SC), a civil engineering, architectural, and surveying firm, merged into **DSAtlantic Corp.** (Raleigh, NC), an employee-owned full-service engineering, architectural, and surveying firm. The combined firm decided to operated under the DSAtlantic name.

Robert Bein, William Frost & Associates, Inc. (RBF) (Irvine, CA), a 350-employee planning, environmental analysis, engineering, and surveying firm, acquired 20-person **Urban Design Studio** (San Juan Capistrano, CA) and 60-person environmental consulting firm **Michael Brandman Associates** (San Jose, CA).

GA Environmental Services, Inc. (GA) (Eddystone, PA), a 50-person environmental and engineering consulting firm, purchased 100% of the stock of **Raritian Enviro Sciences, Inc. (RES)** (East Brunswick, NJ), a 25-person environmental consulting firm. RES agreed to retain its name and function as a wholly owned subsidiary of GA.

Thermo TerraTech, Inc. (Waltham, MA), a 1,000-person subsidiary of **Thermo Electron, Inc.** (Waltham, MA), acquired **Carlan Consulting Group** (Pensacola, FL), a 75-person transportation and environmental consulting, engineering, and architectural firm. Carlan agreed to operate as a division of Thermo TerraTech subsidiary **Killam Associates** (Millburn, NJ) and was renamed Carlan Killam Consulting Group.

January 1997

GEI Consultants, Inc. (Winchester, MA), a 180-person geotechnical firm, acquired 70-person environmental consulting firm **Atlantic Environmental Services, Inc.** (Colchester, CT).

February 1997

Century Engineering (Towson, MD), a 200-person consulting engineering firm, was sold by its parent firm, **Riparius Corp.** (Timonium, MD), to private investor Francis X. Smyth. Smyth became CEO of Century, while the rest of the management team stayed in place.

Kimley-Horn & Associates, Inc. (Raleigh, NC), a 750-person consulting engineering firm, acquired **Jennlyn International** (Boulder, CO), a 20-person consulting engineering firm.

Buena Engineers (Las Vegas, NV), a 12-person environmental and geotechnical firm, and **Geofon, Inc.** (Diamond Bar, CA), a 35-person environmental engineering and design-build firm, merged to form **Buena-Geofon, Inc.** (Las Vegas, NV). The merger provided Geofon with enhanced geotechnical, construction materials testing, and inspection engineering services.

Woolpert (Dayton, OH), a 630-person full-service E/A firm, acquired **WHGK** (Belleville, IL), a 15-person architecture firm.

March 1997

Professional Service Industries (PSI) (Lombard, IL), a 3,000-employee environmental consulting, geotechnical engineering, and construction testing firm, made two acquisitions. PSI acquired 35-person construction materials testing, geotechnical engineering, and environmental services firm **GeoEnvironmental & Materials, Inc.** (Tempe, AZ). PSI also acquired **Pacific Testing Laboratories, Inc.** (Seattle, WA), a 75-person construction materials testing and geotechical engineering firm.

Tomahawk II, Inc. (San Diego, CA), a subsidiary of **Tomahawk Corp.** (Calgary, Alberta), acquired 30-person civil engineering, document conversion, and geotechnical firm **Apex Group** (San Diego, CA).

Merrick & Company (Denver, CO), a 550-person E/A and environmental consulting firm, acquired 15-person environmental consulting firm **Santa Fe Engineering Ltd.** (Santa Fe, NM).

Mid-Kansas Engineering Consultants, Inc. (Wichita, KS) acquired six-person **Hartwell-Jantz Engineering** (Wichita, KS).

Foster Wheeler Environmental Corp. (Lyndhurst, NJ) acquired 16-person **Hartman Associates, Inc.** (Seattle, WA), and renamed it **Hartman Consulting Corp.**

Where to Find Buyers and Sellers

☑ *If you're looking to sell your firm or buy another firm, knowing where to find potential transaction partners can be half the battle. Here are some places to find lists of firms in the A/E/P and environmental consulting industries.*

ACEC Directory
American Consulting Engineers Council
1015 15th Street, NW, Suite 802
Washington, D.C. 20005
Tel: (202)347-7474
Fax: (202)898-0068
Web site: http://www.acec.org
E-mail: acec@acec.org

Engineering News-Record Directory of Design Firms
The McGraw-Hill Companies, Inc.
1221 Avenue of the Americas
Room 4188
New York, New York 10020
Tel: (212)512-4635
Fax: (212)512-4178

Environmental Services Directory
Northeast • Southeast • West Central
Midwest • Pacific West
Environmental Information, Ltd.
4801 West 81st Street, Suite 119
Minneapolis, MN 55437
Tel: (612)831-2473
Fax: (612)831-6550
Web site: http://www..envirobiz.com
E-mail: ei@mr.net

International Directory of Consulting Engineers
International Federation of Consulting Engineers
P.O. Box 86
CH-1000 Lausanne 12
Switzerland
Tel: 41 (21) 653-5003
Fax: 41 (21) 653-5432

The New England Environmental Directory
The Environmental Marketing Group, Inc.
1770 Massachusetts Avenue
Cambridge, Massachusetts 02140
Tel: (617)666-6800
Fax: (617)628-7267
Web site: http://www.envirodirectory.com
E-mail: EnviroDir@aol.com or info@envirodirectory.com

ProFile
The Directory of U.S. Architectural Design Firms
Murray Publishing Company
P.O. Box 1402
160 Broad Street
Summit, NJ 07901
Tel: (908)598-9004
Fax: (908)598-9139
E-mail: murraypub@aol.com

World Environmental Directory
951 Pershing Drive
Silver Spring, Maryland 20910-4464
Tel: (301)587-6300
Fax: (301)5871081
Web site: http://www.bpinews.com
E-mail: bpinews@aol.com

The Yellow Pages

The Internet Yellow Pages
http://www.the-yellowpages.com

Additional Sources of Information

☑ *The following are resources for anyone seeking further information on mergers and acquisitions.*

American Society of Appraisers
P.O. Box 17265
Washington, D.C. 20041
Tel: (800)272-8258
Fax: (703)742-8471
Web site: http://www.appraisers.org

Institute of Business Appraisers
P.O. Box 1447
Boynton Beach, FL 33425
Tel: (407)732-3202
Fax: (407)732-4304
E-mail: ibahq@aol.com

Professional Services Management Association (PSMA)
Case Studies on Mergers & Acquisitions
P.O. Box 910
21300 Catawba Avenue
Cornelius, NC 98031
Tel: (704)895-8890
Fax: (704)895-8873

Zweig White & Associates, Inc.
Insider's Guide to Cashing In On Your Equity in an A/E/P or Environmental Consulting Firm
Valuation Survey of A/E/P and Environmental Consulting Firms, 1997 ed.
Principal's Survey of A/E/P and Environmental Consulting Firms, 1997 ed.
Financial Performance Survey of Environmental Consulting Firms, 1996 ed.
600 Worcester Street
Natick, MA 01760
Tel: (508)651-1559
Fax: (508)653-6522
Web site: http://www.zwa.com
E-mail: info@zwa.com

Index

C

D

E

M

N

O

P

S

T

U

V

W

Z

About the Authors

Editors

George E. Christodoulo
Executive Editor
George Christodoulo is a partner in the Corporate Department at Burns & Levinson LLP in Boston, Massachusetts. He has spent over twenty years in private practice in Boston, counseling both private and public established and emerging companies, as well as individual investors, in general corporate, securities, financing and restructuring, mergers and acquisitions, and real estate matters. Mr. Christodoulo has extensive experience in providing legal services to professional service organizations and family-owned businesses, with an emphasis on ownership transition, management succession, and long-term business planning. He has lectured, both regionally and nationally, to various professional associations on these topics and has written extensively on such matters. Burns & Levinson LLP is located at 125 Summer Street, Boston, MA 02110-1624, telephone (617)345-3000 and fax (617)345-3299. Mr. Christodoulo can be reached directly at (617)345-3897.

Molly O. Whelan
Managing Editor
Molly Whelan is a consultant at Zweig White & Associates, Inc. who specializes in firm mergers and acquisitions, employee surveys, market research, process marketing, and management audits for consulting engineering, architecture, and environmental consulting firms. She also serves as a writer for Zweig White & Associates industry publications.

Attorneys of Burns and Levinson LLP

Susan M. Barnard
Sue Barnard is the chairman of Burns & Levinson's Corporate Department. She regularly represents clients in corporate acquisitions, dispositions, contracts, and other corporate law matters. Her expertise includes rendering securities law advice on both initial and secondary public offerings and private debt and equity financings.

Dana C. Blakslee
Dana Blakslee is a corporate partner. He has extensive experience in the mergers, acquisitions, and dispositions of closely held businesses. He has represented clients in various types of domestic and international transactions.

Robert C. Rives, Jr.
Robert Rives, a corporate partner, represents public and private companies, with an emphasis on emerging growth companies. His expertise includes the licensing and protection of intellectual property, trade secrets, and franchising.

Martin B. Shulkin
A corporate attorney, Martin Shulkin concentrates his practice in mergers and acquisitions and reorganizations of closely held and family-owned businesses. He represents clients in various areas of businesses, including high technology, manufacturing, retail, and professional practices.

Norman C. Spector
Norman Spector is chairman of Burns & Levinson's Finance and Creditor's Rights Department. He represents lenders and borrowers in the structuring, negotiation, and documentation of commercial transactions. Mr. Spector also represents privately held businesses, which includes advising both the business and the owners in acquisitions and sales.

Melvin A. Warsaw
A tax partner, Melvin Warsaw advises private businesses and public corporations on how to structure strategic acquisitions and expansion, the sale of a business, choice of entity, and other operating decisions. He regularly advises foundations and executives of start-up and other private companies concerning the tax aspects of equity and cash compensation programs available for growing businesses, as well as ownership transition and long-term financial planning.

Consultants of Zweig White & Associates, Inc.

Michael "Mick" E. Morrissey
Currently Mick Morrissey is a principal at ZWA and leads the firm's U.S. and international merger and acquisition practice, in addition to conducting management audits and strategic business planning sessions for the design and environmental service professions. He is both a civil engineer and a management consultant with over ten years experience working in and consulting to firms in the A/E/P and environmental consulting industries. Mr. Morrissey can be reached at Zweig White & Associates, telephone (508)651-1559.

Mark C. Zweig
Mark Zweig, who founded Zweig White & Associates, Inc. (ZWA) in 1988, is a leading expert in management for the A/E/P and environmental consulting industries. As president of ZWA, he consults to top management in A/E/P and Environmental Consulting firms throughout the U.S. in strategic planning, turnarounds, organization restructuring, mergers and acquisitions, marketing, operations, finance and human resources.

Frederick D. White
As Executive Vice President of Zweig White & Associates, Fred White is responsible for general project oversight and manages the day-to-day activities of the firm. As consultant, he specializes in firm mergers and acquisitions, marketing strategies, market research, marketing information systems, and high-level executive search for the architecture, consulting engineering, and environmental consulting professions.

Jonathan D. Gatti
Jon Gatti is a consultant who specializes in firm mergers and acquisitions, management audits, and research analysis for consulting engineering, architecture, and environmental consulting firms. In addition, he serves as the administrator of the ZWEIG 100 financial index, and the editor of ZWA's *Merger & Acquisition Advisor.*

Mark J. Goodale
Mark Goodale is a management consultant who specializes in employee surveys, firm mergers and acquisitions, market research, and management audits for A/E/P and environmental consulting firm clients. He is a regular contributor to *The Zweig Letter* and the *Merger & Acquisition Advisor*, published by ZWA.

Jerome "Jerry" A. Guerra

Jerry Guerra's specialties include writing and editing, publishing, marketing consulting, interviewing, sales, and promotion. He is the editor of *The Zweig Letter,* a weekly management newsletter for the design and environmental consulting industries and is also responsible for editing *The Zweig Letter Audio Edition.*

Philip "Chip" C. Horowitz, ASA

Chip Horowitz is a financial analyst, business appraiser, and civil engineer with over 18 years experience in the engineering and financial communities. A principal at ZWA, he specializes in firm mergers and acquisitions, business valuation, ownership transition planning, and financial analysis for the design and environmental consulting professions. He also serves as project manager for the ZWEIG 100 financial index.